MUSTAFA
KEMAL
ATATÜRK

SERIES EDITOR: Bonnie G. Smith, Rutgers University

THE LIVES OF PEOPLE and the unfolding of earth-shaking events inspire us to love history. We live in a global age where big concepts such as globalization often tempt us to forget the people side of the past. The titles in *The World in a Life* series aim to revive these meaningful lives. Each one shows us what it felt like to live on a world stage and even to shape the world's destiny.

The lives of most individuals are full of activity and color and even passion and violence. The people examined in *The World in a Life* series often faced outsized challenges, but they usually met the great events of their day energetically. They lived amid enormous change, as we often do. Their lives show us how to navigate change and to find solutions. They made fateful decisions, often with much soul searching or—as often—on the spur of the moment and even intuitively. We have much to learn from these fateful past lives.

Their actions, however, were filled with complexity. Biographies in this series give a "nutshell" explanation of how important paradoxes and dilemmas have been in the stories of individuals operating on the world stage. Their lives become windows onto the complicated trends, events, and crises of their time, providing an entry point for a deeper understanding of a particular historical era. As such events and crises unfolded, these historical figures also faced crises in their personal lives. In the intertwined dramas of the personal and political, of the individual and the global, we come to understand the complexities of acting on the world stage and living in world history.

BONNIE G. SMITH

MUSTAFA KEMAL ATATÜRK

HEIR TO AN EMPIRE

RYAN GINGERAS

New York   Oxford
OXFORD UNIVERSITY PRESS

Oxford University Press is a department of the University of Oxford.
It furthers the University's objective of excellence in research,
scholarship, and education by publishing worldwide.

Oxford   New York
Auckland   Cape Town   Dar es Salaam   Hong Kong   Karachi
Kuala Lumpur   Madrid   Melbourne   Mexico City   Nairobi
New Delhi   Shanghai   Taipei   Toronto

With offices in
Argentina   Austria   Brazil   Chile   Czech Republic   France   Greece
Guatemala   Hungary   Italy   Japan   Poland   Portugal   Singapore
South Korea   Switzerland   Thailand   Turkey   Ukraine   Vietnam

For titles covered by Section 112 of the US Higher Education
Opportunity Act, please visit www.oup.com/us/he for the
latest information about pricing and alternate formats.

Published by Oxford University Press
198 Madison Avenue, New York, New York 10016
http://www.oup.com

Library of Congress Cataloging-in-Publication Data
Gingeras, Ryan.
    Mustafa Kemal Atatürk : heir to an empire / Ryan Gingeras (Naval
Postgraduate School).
        pages cm. -- (The World in a Life)
    Includes bibliographical references and index.
    ISBN 978-0-19-025001-0 (paperback : acid-free paper) 1. Atatürk,
Kemal, 1881-1938. 2. Atatürk, Kemal, 1881-1938--Influence. 3. Presidents--
Turkey--Biography. 4. Soldiers--Turkey--Biography. 5. Revolutionaries--
Turkey--Biography. 6. Turkey--Politics and government--1918-1960.
7. Turkey--History--1918-1960. I. Title.
    DR592.K4G54 2016
    956.1'024092--dc23
    [B]
                                                                2015008407

Printing number: 9 8 7 6 5 4 3 2 1

Printed in the United States of America
on acid-free paper

CONTENTS

LIST OF ILLUSTRATIONS

LIST OF MAPS

ACKNOWLEDGMENTS

I FIRST WANT TO THANK Bonnie Smith, Priscilla McGeehon, and Charles Cavaliere for the opportunity and guidance in writing and producing this book. It is genuinely an honor and a privilege to be given the chance to write a book like this. Being presented with the opportunity to write about Atatürk along the lines of *The World in a Life* series was an exceptional treat and honor. I want to thank my colleagues at the Naval Postgraduate School who encouraged me to take on the project and offered advice. I want to thank my friends and colleagues in the field who have supported my work and offered needed pointers on how to put a biography like this together. Through taking on this project, I have a greater appreciation for those who have tried to encapsulate the life of Mustafa Kemal in a thoughtful way. I realize now how difficult it is to thoroughly and astutely render his life in its entirety. For this reason I am very much indebted to the scholarship of Paul Dumont, Şükrü Hanioğlu, Klaus Kreiser, and Andrew Mango. As always, I am most grateful for the love and support of my family. I would like to dedicate this book to my children, Amaya and Sebastian, the two greatest people I will ever know.

ABOUT THE AUTHOR

RYAN GINGERAS is an associate professor in the National Security Affairs Department in the Naval Postgraduate School in Monterey, California. He is the author of *Sorrowful Shores: Violence, Ethnicity, and the End of the Ottoman Empire*, which received short-list distinctions for the *Rothschild Book Prize in Nationalism and Ethnic Studies* and the *British-Kuwait Friendship Society Book Prize*. He is also the author of *Heroin, Organized Crime and the Making of Modern Turkey*. He has published on a wide variety of topics related to history and politics in such journals as *International Journal of Middle East Studies, Middle East Journal, Iranian Studies, Diplomatic History, Past & Present,* and *Journal of Contemporary European History*.

INTRODUCTION

THE REPUBLIC OF TURKEY is a young country born out of the tumult of the early twentieth century. Its establishment in 1923 was a consequence of the long and tortured demise of the Ottoman Empire, a state that was over six centuries old at the time of its passing. Like modern Russia, China, Iran, and Austria, Turkey inherited a complicated and bitter legacy from its imperial antecedent. At the dawn of the twentieth century, the Ottoman Empire was diplomatically isolated, politically unstable, socially fractious, and economically weak. The new century brought all of these weaknesses and insecurities to the fore. During the course of ten years of hard fighting (a period which also includes the very worst of World War I), hundreds of thousands of the empire's citizens perished from war, famine, and state oppression. The egregious suffering of the Ottoman people, as well its defeat at the hands of Britain and France, impugned the early Turkish state from the start. For many, the fall of the Ottoman sultans, like the demise of the Romanovs, the Habsburgs, the Hollenzollerns, and the Qing, represented more than a just and overdue end. Turkey's Ottoman heritage was a mark of backwardness and villainy.

Turkey's political fortunes turned rapidly within ten years of its founding. By the late 1930s, international commentators greeted the country's development as nothing short of a modern marvel. In contrast to the empire it replaced, Turkey quickly grew into a visibly stronger, more stable, and ostensibly more enlightened state. The laws propagated from Ankara were progressively committed to the reformation of society and the building of an administration worthy of international esteem. Like other postwar powers, the country's political ethos was grounded in a rousingly proud and uncompromising form of nationalism. Its ultra-secular leaders prided themselves in their embrace of contemporary European motifs and social tastes. Despite the Great Depression, Turkey's economy managed to recover from much of the damage the Ottoman Empire sustained during World War I. While by no means a land of great riches, Turkey was distinctively more independent and economically vibrant than its imperial predecessor. By the outbreak of World War II, the Republic of Turkey epitomized more than a state bound for better times; Turkey, like Italy or the Soviet Union, aspired to represent the essence of modern politics in the twentieth century.

To contemporaries of this period, Mustafa Kemal Atatürk, the country's first president, was both the muse and architect of this radical transformation. By the time of his death in 1938, he was regularly compared alongside other luminary statesmen of the post-Versailles era. Outside of Turkey, his name was synonymous with both bold leadership and ambitious reform. He demonstrably played the role of the country's savior well. Mustafa Kemal impressed his fellow citizens and foreign guests as a man driven by vivaciousness and confidence. Atatürk's reputation as a man both progressive and iconoclastic greatly augmented his already lofty status as Turkey's premier general and war hero. His acclaim and celebrity manifested in the West and the East. Even before his untimely death, he had earned the praise of European and American leaders as well as nationalists and religious leaders in Asia and the Middle East. Like a modern Peter the Great or Emperor Meiji, Atatürk embodied the notion that even the most torpid or defeated nation could be redeemed and remade under the guidance of an inspired, enlightened, and commanding leader.

Some aspects of his presidency did temper the admiration Mustafa Kemal gleaned at home and abroad. He was undeniably a dictator with little patience for liberal democracy. His penchant for self-promotion helped to create a servile political culture that deviated little from his dictums and values. Atatürk's inability to brook compromise and tolerate opposition also engendered acts of violence and oppression that resulted in the deaths of large numbers of his fellow citizens. On a personal level, the "Gazi," as many affectionately called him, developed a reputation for scandal and impropriety. His tumultuous relationships with women, and his love of drink, often left him exposed to gossip and expressions of unease.

An understanding of the life and times of Mustafa Kemal Atatürk is an essential first step to understanding the complexities of the modern Turkish Republic. In surveying his life, one encounters an encapsulation of the core events that shaped the country's metamorphosis from aging empire to a young nation-state. His trials and tribulations, beginning with his childhood, provide key insights into the most dominant political and social themes of his era. A great many of the issues Atatürk struggled with, such as secularism, national identity, Western relations, and modernity, are all issues that present-day Turks continue to confront as matters of state and society.

There is very little about Mustafa Kemal's upbringing and early career that fundamentally determined his rise to global fame and recognition. Much of his youth was confined to a fairly cosmopolitan, but still provincial, portion of the Ottoman Empire. His decision to pursue a military education assured his passage out of his Balkan hometown of Salonika. Atatürk spent the majority of his life as an officer in the Ottoman army. He fought in virtually every war that marked the empire's eventual collapse. He developed an early reputation for valor and steely leadership. In defeating the armies of Greece, Britain, and France during the course of Turkey's self-proclaimed war of liberation, Mustafa Kemal assumed an unassailable political position within the country. Yet behind the veneer of his military feats, he revealed himself to be a man with great political ambitions and profound intellectual curiosities. His acumen for ideas and debate, as well as his deep-seated desire for power, eventually became Atatürk's most important assets as his career shifted toward politics.

His first years in office were precarious and bloody. Atatürk began his tenure as Turkey's president with a series of primary structural reforms aimed at building a strong state with him at the helm. He could be a merciless political opponent, as demonstrated by his fierce campaigns against political contenders in the capital and rebels in the countryside. As Mustafa Kemal's hold on power grew more certain, the tempo and severity of his reforms escalated precipitously. Under the auspices of his intellectual tutelage and unquestioned political authority, a cultural revolution swept over the republic. The changes wrought were generally aimed at replacing institutions and practices associated with the supposed failures of the Ottoman Empire. In supplanting old imperial norms with explicitly Westernized customs and conventions, Atatürk hoped to leave for future generations a state that would not succumb to defeat or collapse.

Turkey's continued endurance into the twentieth century still inspires many to adore him as the country's eternal leader. Yet in urging Turkish society to conform to his vision of a modern, progressive nation, he also sowed seeds of discontent and distrust, prompting many contemporary Turks to still harbor ill will toward Atatürk's legacy. What remains beyond dispute is that Atatürk's life and achievements remain the touchstone of the republic he constructed and guided out of its troubled origins. His vision of Turkey as a state and nation still frames how contemporary Turks imagine both the present and future of the country.

CHAPTER 1

| ATATÜRK AS A YOUNG MAN, |
1880–1912

IN JANUARY 1922, Mustafa Kemal Atatürk offered a chief corre-
spondent from an Istanbul newspaper an opportunity to speak
at length about his life and career. The interview touched upon
numerous subjects related to his early education, his family, his
first years in the military, and his political leanings as a young
man. This lengthy discussion of his life was the first time Mustafa
Kemal had publicly attempted to explain and contextualize his
ascendency as a general in the Ottoman army and leader of the
so-called National Movement to liberate the empire from foreign
occupation. The revelations found within the interview are significant when one considers the context and timing of its publication. By that winter, Mustafa Kemal appeared to be on the
threshold of securing an independent and solidified state in what
had been the Ottoman Empire's central provinces in Anatolia.
His status as the supreme political leader of Turkey, as well as
his rise to international prominence as a symbol of anti-imperial
resistance, would be affirmed almost two years later with the
establishment of the Republic of Turkey and his election to the
post of president. Thereafter, it is clear that his fame and political
weight colored much of Mustafa Kemal's candidness about his
ideas and experiences.

Mustafa Kemal composed no autobiography. After becoming president, he imparted to friends and acquaintances only a few anecdotes drawn from his youth. Most of the recollections he divulged over the later part of his life concerned his experiences in World War I, the Turkish War of Independence, and the early days of the Turkish Republic. Many friends and family members, including a few who knew him as a youth, later added to these stories in their own memoirs or in interviews. However, Mustafa Kemal's subsequent fame clearly influenced the content of these recollections, often transforming him, even at an early age, into an incorruptible and undaunted leader and thinker.

For these reasons, it is difficult to render and corroborate various details of Mustafa Kemal's early life. In surveying the resources available, it is often difficult to separate reality from the myths and legends that have formed around his upbringing and early experiences. An equally formidable challenge confronting biographers and scholars is the relative obscurity of the cultural, political, and societal traits that informed Mustafa Kemal's life. Few today in Turkey, for example, can read and understand the writings and speeches delivered by Mustafa Kemal in Ottoman Turkish, which differs dramatically from the language of the modern republic. The world in which Mustafa Kemal lived generally bears little resemblance to contemporary Turkey. Understanding and contextualizing the incredible physical and human diversity of the Ottoman Empire, as well as its deeply layered, intricate and contradictory political system, poses a difficult challenge for scholars and amateur historians alike.

With these limitations in mind, a survey of Mustafa Kemal's early life does offer important insights into both the makings of this future leader and the influences that impacted the various peoples and nations that have been shaped by the Ottoman Empire. A closer look at his maturation into a mid-ranking officer provides several examples that represent core themes that would define his career as both a soldier and a statesman. Perhaps more important, a deeper understanding of Mustafa Kemal's youth affirms that he was not a unique or peerless individual. The trials and achievements seen in his childhood, schooling, and early professional life resonate strongly in the lives of many figures who played major and minor roles in the unmaking of the Ottoman Empire and the building of the Republic of Turkey.

Many have noted, often with some irony, that the man who fancied himself the "Father of the Turks" was technically neither born nor raised in the land he claimed as the historic home of his ethnic kin. Mustafa Kemal Atatürk's most formative experiences were instead shaped by the peoples, politics, and history of southeastern Europe. Indeed, one may say that his story, up until the age of twenty-two, is typical of men and women who heralded from this portion of the old Ottoman world. To comprehend Mustafa Kemal as a man, and as a representation of the evolution of the states he would serve and help, one must first survey the evolution of the place of his birth: the city of Salonika. It is against the backdrop of this emerging port located on the Aegean during the late nineteenth century that he would acquire many of the most critical lessons and experiences that helped form his career and his outlook on politics and culture. Mustafa Kemal, until his death in 1938, remained a consummate *Selanikli*, a man from Salonika. Arguably, the culture Atatürk would later attempt to promulgate and embody was hauntingly reminiscent of the trends, mores, and trappings of the city he left behind in his youth. To put it another way, the early Republic of Turkey, in a number of ways, constituted a re-creation of the former lives and aspirations of men like Mustafa Kemal, who were displaced from the European cities and provinces of the Ottoman Empire.

By the time Mustafa was born in 1880 or 1881, Salonika (or Thessaloniki as it is referred to today in Greece) had been a key administrative and economic center of the Ottoman Empire for 450 years. Like other emerging cities on the Mediterranean, such as Beirut, Izmir, and Istanbul, Salonika benefited greatly from the economic and cultural vibrancy associated with transnational trade in the nineteenth century. The steady influx of local and foreign

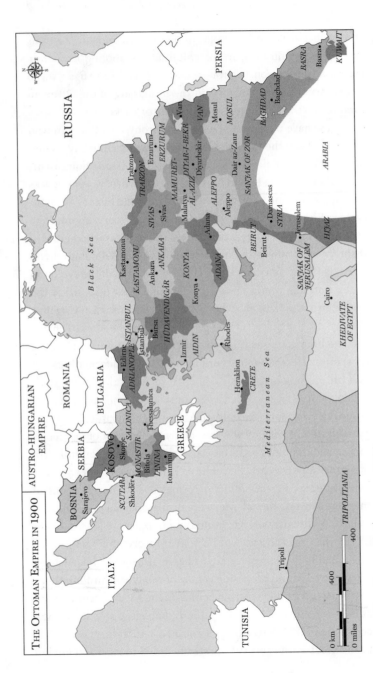

MAP 1. THE OTTOMAN EMPIRE IN 1900

goods and traders into the port transformed the social and economic landscape of the city by the turn of the twentieth century. While still relatively sleepy and provincial compared to the imperial capital, the city of Mustafa Kemal's youth boasted many of the trappings of modern life during this era. A railway line linked Salonika to the train traffic of the Balkans and Central Europe, while aboveground and underwater telegraph cables brought news and directives from Istanbul and the wider world. Unlike many towns in the Ottoman Empire, Salonika's streets and neighborhoods featured streetcars, gas lamps, theaters, cafes, music halls, and shops carrying the latest consumer and luxury wares of the day. The sophistication of Mustafa Kemal's hometown appeared to have imbued its residents with a confidence and a more elevated status compared to those who came from more modest towns or villages in the Balkans and Anatolia. The city's proximity to the capital, coupled with its vital role as an Ottoman entrepôt to the world economy, tied Salonika closely to the fortunes of the Ottoman state, making it a vital provincial showplace for the empire's increasingly modern political, economic, and social culture.

A traveler visiting Salonika in the late nineteenth century would have found its markets, docks, and street corners populated with individuals speaking many languages and professing a variety of faiths. As the chief port of the southern Balkans, the city's inhabitants reflected the profound cultural diversity of the region; conversations in Turkish, Greek, Albanian, and a host of Slavic languages and dialects were commonplace along the city's streets. Europeans, Americans, and migrants from other parts of the Ottoman Empire also added to this ragu of cultures. Unlike many cities in the empire, Salonika also possessed a large Jewish population that descended directly from the expulsions of fifteenth-century inquisitions in Spain and Portugal. By 1890, Jews represented almost half of the city's population. Muslims, foreign nationals, and Orthodox Christians, respectively, made up the remaining sum of the nearly hundred thousand residents living in Salonika.[1] Several anecdotes suggest that Mustafa Kemal, resident of the city's Sunni Muslim quarter, regularly interacted with neighbors of different ethnic and religious backgrounds. According to one story, he once sought to marry a young Greek girl until he was dissuaded by his uncle. His relationships with the diverse peoples of the city, for the most part however, appear less dramatic. As a young man, Mustafa was known to regularly visit tavernas and cafes frequented by non-Muslims on the waterfront,

11082-Salonica (ancient Thessalonica) S showing ruins, modern city and bay. Copyright Underwood & Underwood. U-13883

A PORT TO THE WORLD: SALONIKA. *Mustafa Kemal reflected the full diversity of the empire and many of the cultural and social trends of the turn of the twentieth century.*

where he would carouse with friends, listen to music in a variety of languages, and, per chance, meet women.

Mustafa Kemal's parents were representative of the complexities and changes that defined nineteenth-century Salonika and the Ottoman Empire at large. His father, Ali Rıza, was the son of a primary school teacher and appeared to have been a native of the city. Like his father before him, he sought a livelihood in the empire's ever-expanding civil bureaucracy as a clerk in a pious foundation (*evkaf*) and as a customs official. Since the beginning of the nineteenth century, Istanbul had hoped to secure the future survival of the empire through the creation of new, centralized, and modern institutions and departments staffed with professional bureaucrats like Ali Rıza. Unfortunately for Mustafa's father, state service did not result in a necessarily lucrative career. As a customs official along the Ottoman-Greek border south of town, Ali also took up trade as a timber merchant to supplement his income. Work along the border, according to family sources, was often dangerous due to the threat of bandits seeking to extort tradesmen and travelers. The profits he did glean from his business dealings, however, did afford him the opportunity to build the three-story house in which Mustafa was born.

Zübeyde, Mustafa Kemal's mother, came from a more traditional background. Her family came from the region of Vodina to the west of Salonika and established themselves as stewards and laborers on land just outside of the city. Twenty years younger than her husband, Zübeyde possessed no formal education. She was also notably more devout than her husband, even though Ali Rıza also came from a family with a strong religious background. Although both Ali and Zübeyde spoke Turkish, the ethnic roots of Mustafa Kemal's parents remain unclear. While he did possess Albanian relatives on his mother's side, Atatürk later claimed to descend from nomadic Turkic tribesmen who settled in the Balkans during the early centuries of Ottoman rule in the region. Regardless of the ethnic origins of his parents, Mustafa undoubtedly identified himself primarily as a Sunni Muslim. It was only later, with his gradual adoption of ethnic nationalism as a corner-stone for the Republic of Turkey, that his ethnic identity as a Turk, real or imagined, came to the fore.

Mustafa was one of two children Zübeyde bore who survived childhood. At the age of seven or eight, his father also passed away, leaving the family in precarious straits. His widowed mother re-located her family outside Salonika to the family farm near her native town of Langaza (today the Greek municipality of Langadas). After a brief stay, she returned with her children to Salonika and eventually remarried. Her second husband, Ragıp, was a widower and worked as a clerk with the state's tobacco monopoly. After she remarried, Zübeyde's relationship with her son often appears to have been fractious. Nevertheless, Mustafa remained a commit-ted and loyal son and eventually reconciled with his stepfather. His devotion to his mother grew stronger as further hardship befell her in later years.

Mustafa Kemal's first memory, according to the recollections he imparted in 1922, concerned his parent's dispute over what kind of education he would receive as a child. Zübeyde, the more religious of the two, hoped her son would receive a traditional clerical education at a local mosque. His father, however, insisted that he attend a more secular school run by a progressive educator named Şemsi Efendi. Initially his mother's wishes were fulfilled, but, after a few days, Mustafa entered Şemsi Efendi's French-influenced school. Many of Atatürk's biographers have found special significance in this moment of his life. Mustafa Kemal's brief exposure as a child to Western, secular education fore-shadows his later devotion to unorthodox, revolutionary, and foreign ideas. More important, this short chapter in his life is symbolic of the deeper intellectual and cultural tensions that defined the Ottoman Empire during the nineteenth century. The positions his parents took on Mustafa's education, for many scholars, represent two poles within popular and elitist thinking regarding the Ottoman state and its future. On the one hand, Zübeyde's preference for a clerical education has been interpreted as symbolic of conservative Ottoman political tendencies that sought to maintain the empire's traditional institutions (such as the sultanate and preeminence of Islam as a source of legal and political inspiration). On the other hand, Ali Rıza's inclination

THE MATRIARCH OF A HERO. *Zübeyde, Mustafa Kemal's mother, remained close to him until her death in 1924.*

toward a secular schooling seems to reflect the increasingly dominant political ideology of the empire's young elite during the nineteenth century. The curriculum of Şemsi Efendi's school, which emphasized critical thinking and secular knowledge, resonated strongly with many civil servants, like Ali Rıza, who saw Western-inspired education as key to rejuvenating and maintaining the Ottoman Empire in the modern era.

The death of his father, as well as his brief displacement to Langaza, cut short Mustafa's first years in school. When he eventually returned to Salonika, his mother placed him in a local civil service school. Her son detested his new school, particularly after a teacher beat the young man for fighting with his classmates. At the age of thirteen, he took the state exam to enter a local military school. His decision, which was again against his mother's wishes, came as the result of a number of factors. According to Atatürk's own account, the sharp dress of an officer's uniform drew him to soldiering. Three of his younger relatives also took up a military education around the same time (all of whom later became trusted aids when he ascended to the upper ranks of the Ottoman army). More profoundly, service in the sultan's army had become, by the late nineteenth century, a favored profession of many young Muslim men living throughout the empire. At a time when commerce and industry were increasingly dominated by Western investors and traders, opportunities to become a successful merchant appeared to be largely limited to Ottoman Christians and Jews (two groups long associated with transnational trade in the Balkans and elsewhere in the empire). State service, in either the bureaucracy or the military, seemed to offer young, ambitious Muslims greater avenues of personal and financial fulfillment.

Mustafa Kemal's decision to seek a military education, like his early foray into secular, Western schooling, also represents a larger, existential theme that defined the Ottoman Empire during the late nineteenth century. His entrance into the Salonika's military preparatory school signifies to many scholars an inborn patriotism and love toward the Ottoman state. He was undoubtedly conscious of the wars and rebellions that had plagued the empire since the start of the century and was aware of the fragile state of the empire's political future in the 1880s and 1890s. Only two or three years before his birth, the empire's loss in the Russo-Ottoman War of 1878 had resulted in the partition of large sections of Istanbul's holdings in the Balkans and prompted hundreds of thousands of Muslim refugees to relocate to what remained of the empire. Mustafa Kemal's induction into military life starkly contrasted with the overwhelming non-Muslim and mercantile nature of his native city. Orthodox Christians and Jews in Salonika and elsewhere typically did not enter the military or bureaucracy but found their fortunes in trade and business. More important, Ottoman Christians were often the chief architects and beneficiaries of the nationalist insurrections that had resulted in the suffering and territorial losses that had beset the empire. Many Muslims also perceived Christian merchants and intellectuals as collaborators with Western states that had helped foster the empire's hardships. The Ottoman press of Mustafa Kemal's youth often invoked the saying that "Non-Muslims have European protectors; we have no protector but God."[2] His decision, in the grander scheme of things, was more than just an act of rational self-interest. Taking up the standard of the Ottoman military appears to have been a pledge of fealty to the state, one that, in the view of many of his contemporaries and modern biographers, set him apart from his non-Muslim neighbors and fellow citizens.

Mustafa excelled in his primary school studies, ultimately graduating fourth in his class in 1898. It was as a student in Salonika that he earned his second name, Kemal ("perfection" in Arabic), which many claimed denoted his acumen as a student. After graduation, he chose to continue his military education at a high school located to the north of Salonika in the town of Manastır (today, the city of Bitola in the Republic of Macedonia). While possessing a modicum of Salonika's urbanity, Manastır's political and social climate was markedly more tense and violent. In the two decades preceding his arrival to this inland Macedonian town, communal conflict in the region had rapidly escalated as Orthodox Christian revolutionaries sought to undermine Ottoman authority and agitate the local peasantry into revolt. Paramilitary gangs (called *çetes* in Turkish) controlled large portions of Macedonia's rough countryside. Tahsin Uzer, a fellow native of Salonika and later an administrator in the province, recalled that "In every part of Macedonia, battles between Turkish military units and Bulgarian, Greek and Serb *çetes* occurred almost every day."[3] During the year he lived in town, Mustafa Kemal palpably felt the threats of violence, revolt, and partition. When war broke out with Greece in 1897, patriotic fervor compelled him, along with many of his classmates, to attempt to enlist. The brevity of the war, or perhaps his mother's intercession, prevented him from volunteering. Nevertheless, during the decade following Mustafa's graduation from high school in 1899, Manastır and the Macedonian hinterlands at large remained embroiled in communal warfare and dissident nationalism.

Academic success in high school allowed Mustafa an opportunity to attend the imperial war college in Istanbul. The Harbiye, as the college was known, was among the centerpieces of imperial state education during the nineteenth century. Those who entered it were counted among the most elite students of the empire, young men who would later be trusted to not only defend the state from its enemies but also carry on the spirit of reform and modernization initiated during the early 1800s. Mustafa Kemal's first years in the Ottoman capital were both exciting and impactful. By his own admission, his first year was filled with "naïve youthful reveries" such as drinking, dancing, and socializing late into the night.[4] At the Harbiye, he made lifelong friendships with men who later served with and under him in the Ottoman army. While some of his friends came from more established or wealthier backgrounds, each of his close classmates during his youth, such as Ömer Naci, Nuri Conker, Kazım Özalp, Ali Fuat Cebesoy, and Ali Fethi Okyar, were cast from the same mold: they were young, curious, and ambitious Muslim men driven by a deep sense of patriotism. The bonds Mustafa Kemal forged with these early comrades, as well as other young officers and officials in subsequent years, became critical to his later advancement within the military and essential to his political ascendency as president of the young Turkish Republic.

His education at the Harbiye was rigorous and demanding. Staffed by Ottoman and European instructors, the curriculum of the academy was grounded in mathematics, science, European languages, and military studies. Mustafa Kemal, who had already achieved some level of fluency in French before coming to Istanbul, again excelled in the classroom, graduating fifth out of a class of forty-three in 1904. His education and experiences at the Harbiye instilled Mustafa and his classmates with a new sense of privilege and responsibility. The lessons imparted at the academy, as well as the opportunity to live, work, and play within the confines of the imperial capital, inculcated him and his fellow newly minted officers with the notion that the fate of the Ottoman state rested in their hands. One of Atatürk's biographers, Şükrü Hanioğlu, points in particular to the influence German political thought had upon Mustafa Kemal and other graduates of the Harbiye. As leaders of a so-called "nation-in-arms," the Harbiye's students were called upon to heed the advice of the famed military theorist Colmar von der Goltz to assume a "superior position in the state" and guide both government and society through the impending wars that would test the nation's survival.[5]

Important lessons Mustafa Kemal acquired during his school years in both Manastır and Istanbul were propagated outside the classroom. His entrance into the ranks of the Ottoman military came during the reign of Sultan Abdülhamid II. Abdülhamid II ascended to the throne during a momentous period in the empire's history. Shortly after taking power in the fall of 1876, he approved the imposition of a new constitutional order that entailed the creation of a parliament made up of representatives from throughout the Ottoman lands. His compliance with the new regime proved fleeting when, as result of the outbreak of civil unrest in Bulgaria in 1877, Abdülhamid suspended both the parliament and the constitution. Following the end of this first brief constitutional period, the new sultan imposed a rigid administration that barred political dissent and popular activism. Government censors forbade the publication of independent newspapers and journals and forced many of the constitution's staunchest advocates into exile. A climate of fear and suspicion pervaded Abdülhamid II's rule in Istanbul as the sultan's palace wrested greater amounts of political control away from the empire's bureaucracy. For young aspiring officers like Mustafa Kemal, the reign of Abdülhamid II represented a betrayal of the great reforms that had transformed the Ottoman Empire over the previous decades. His propensity toward autocracy, under the auspices of the sultan's age-old prerogatives as ruler of the empire and leader of the Sunni Muslim world, flew in the face of the rational and modern education young cadets like Mustafa Kemal received in their state-run schools and academies. To them, the empire under Abdülhamid II seemed closer to ruin and collapse than at any prior point in their lifetime.

Before coming to Istanbul, one of Mustafa Kemal's earliest friends, Ömer Naci, had exposed him to the writings of Namık Kemal, a journalist and intellectual who was among the key influences of the "Young Ottoman" reformers who crafted the empire's constitution. His famous poem, "The Fatherland's Poem," provided inspiration to Mustafa and others to seek a career in the military. In the conclusion of the poem, Namık declared that:

> Wounds are medals on the brave's body;
> The grave is the soldier's highest rank;
> The earth is the same, above and underneath;
> March, you brave ones, to defend the fatherland.[6]

Early on in his tenure at the Harbiye, Mustafa Kemal, like many of his classmates, sensed that an ill wind had descended upon the capital. Spies and informers with ties to the palace followed the movements of students at the school. Moreover, the writings of earlier reformers, particularly Namık Kemal, were banned, which forced Mustafa and his classmates to read his works in secret. "There seemed to be something wrong in the state," Mustafa recalled in 1922, "if those who read such patriotic works were under surveillance. But we could not completely grasp the essence of it."[7]

Government censorship and scrutiny compelled Mustafa and some of his closest friends to form a clandestine circle committed to dissident ideas. He, along with Ömer Naci, briefly composed a newspaper critical of government policy, an act that nearly resulted in Mustafa Kemal's dismissal from the academy. Involvement in dissident activities again landed Mustafa Kemal in trouble with authorities soon after graduation, which resulted in his detention in prison (although it is not clear if his imprisonment lasted a few days or a few months). Despite his transgressions, he was allowed to remain in the army and retain his rank. Much to his disappointment, his first post in the military did not take him back to Macedonia. Instead, in January 1905, he boarded a ship bound for Ottoman Syria, where he would assume the duties of a staff officer in Damascus.

Mustafa Kemal's stay in Ottoman Syria lasted two-and-a-half years. His duties as a staff officer attached to the empire's Fifth Army in part entailed supporting state security operations aimed at restive elements of the region's population. Most notably, he took part in campaigns against Druze raiders located to the south of Damascus. Military operations like those conducted against the Druze of southern Syria were commonplace in various corners of the Ottoman Empire during the turn of the century; banditry and raiding, particularly at the hands of nomads, displaced migrants, and other socially marginal groups, was endemic to rural life and was counted among the chief threats to law and order. Training missions took Mustafa Kemal to other portions of the Levant as well, such as Jaffa, Beirut, Jerusalem, and Beersheba.

Atatürk's biographers tend to depict these years in his life as an extended period of exile as a result of his political activism while in the Harbiye. By all accounts, Mustafa Kemal did not take well to life in Syria. Living in a dirty, uncomfortable home in Damascus, he longed to return to Salonika. In his own writings and recollections, he made no reference to the Arab neighbors, comrades, or acquaintances he encountered during his time in Syria. Some scholars have surmised that his experiences in the empire's Arab lands clashed with his tastes and feelings as a Turkish-speaking officer. "Oriental" Damascus could not be compared to the "European" progressive charms of Salonika.

His interest in politics did not fade following the reprimands he received in Istanbul. In Damascus, he met a former student of the Ottoman Medical Academy, Mustafa Cantekin, who was exiled to Syria for his involvement in dissident activism. Together they established a secret organization called the Fatherland and Freedom Society in the fall of 1905. In addition to his military duties, Mustafa Kemal invested much of his energies into growing his small circle of conspirators into a network of like-minded dissenters. After establishing contacts in other towns in Ottoman Syria, he received permission to take leave from his unit and journeyed back to Salonika under the pretense of seeking medical treatment. Back in his hometown, he established a small branch of his organization.

The Fatherland and Freedom Society, despite Mustafa Kemal's efforts, did not take root in Salonika and was dissolved following his acceptance of a new post as a staff officer in Salonika in October 1907. By that point in time, another dissident organization, one with a great many more members and greater appeal, began to make inroads among segments of the state's bureaucracy and officer corps in multiple portions of the empire. The Committee of Union and Progress (or CUP, as it later became known), first came into existence in the Ottoman Medical Academy in 1889. Inspired by the writings of "Young Turk" dissident intellectuals based in Paris, the earliest members of the CUP called for a restoration of the 1876 constitution and an end to the autocracy of Abdülhamid II's rule. Following an attempted coup in 1896, government authorities rounded up the organization's members. The CUP's members based in Europe maintained the spirit of the organization in exile following the 1896 plot. Despite deep ideological divisions and the defection of some of the CUP's earliest supporters, a united organization of dissidents rallied together to form a collective front in the hopes of forcing Abdülhamid II to reinstate constitutional rule. At the forefront of the CUP's revived fortunes was a network of officers and bureaucrats based in Ottoman Macedonia. This internally based faction, initially dubbed the Ottoman Freedom Society, was established in 1906 independently of the CUP. However, the groups eventually merged with the much larger and older CUP in 1907. Following the amalgamation of these two wings of the pro-constitutional movement, the CUP's ranks grew stronger within its new base inside the empire's Macedonian provinces. Mustafa Kemal, who had aspired to be among the leaders of the anti-Hamidian cause, joined the CUP at some point before February 1908.

At the time he pledged his loyalty to the CUP, paramilitary violence had intensified dramatically in the Macedonian interior. Between 1903 and 1908, fighting between government forces and various nationalist *çete* formations of Bulgarians, Serbs, Macedonians, and Greeks had claimed tens of thousands of lives and left scores of villages burned and abandoned. Meanwhile, the Great Powers of Europe had endeavored to intervene into the region's provincial affairs in the hopes of reforming the region's security services and bringing about good governance to the war-racked countryside. From the perspective of Ottoman officers stationed in the field, the threat of both insurrection and greater European involvement in Macedonia bore all the signs of potential partition. In the words of the Ahmet Niyazi, one of the earliest and most prominent members of the CUP's branch in Macedonia, "the same sickness that infected Anatolia, the Arab lands, and Libya also was found in Macedonia."[8] The only

Kalağası sütbesinde (Kd. yüzbaşı)

A NEWLY MINTED CAPTAIN. *When he graduated, Atatürk was commissioned as a staff officer in the imperial army.*

solution to the crisis, in the minds of Niyazi and other self-fashioned "Young Turk" leaders in the region, was revolution. Over the first six months of 1908, CUP supporters labored to agitate among fellow officials, officers, landowners, intellectuals, and tradesmen to support an armed insurrection aimed at restoring the parliament and the constitution. The CUP's mobilization efforts also drew in supporters from Christian nationalist groups inside and outside Macedonia who, from their collective perspective, equally suffered under the depredations of Abdülhamid II's rule. "Without exception," as Ahmet Niyazi later put it, "all of us were crushed under the same authoritarian oppression."[9]

In July 1908, Mustafa Kemal was appointed to serve as an inspector on the central railway line that bisected the empire's Macedonian provinces. His service along this vital railroad linking Salonika with the interior occurred within weeks of the outbreak of the CUP's long anticipated revolt. Beginning on July 3, several detachments of Ottoman soldiers left their barracks and took to the hills. With the support of armed bands of civilians in various portions of Macedonia, the rebels telegrammed the sultan and demanded that the constitution be restored. After briefly considering a military response to the mutiny, Abdülhamid II conceded defeat and on July 24 declared his intention to reconvene the parliament. In the wake of the revolt, later dubbed the Young Turk Revolution, celebrations and mass demonstrations in support of the CUP's rebellion erupted spontaneously in various corners of the empire.

Although he did play a role in supplying information and arms to the rebels, Mustafa Kemal was not counted among the so-called "heroes of liberty" whose portraits adorned postcards and posters in the aftermath of the Young Turk Revolution. Alongside Ahmet Niyazi, the most public figure associated with the CUP's victory that summer was a young officer in the Ottoman army named Enver. Enver, similar to Atatürk, was born in 1881 and was the son of a minor state official. Although raised in Istanbul, he too attended the Manastır military academy and graduated from the Harbiye a year after Mustafa Kemal. Yet, unlike the future first president of Turkey, Enver was stationed in Macedonia through his first years in military service. As an infantry officer tasked with pursuing nationalist *çetes*, he forged close ties with many of the key figures who established the CUP's first cells in Macedonia. Although the two men moved in similar circles of friends and comrades, Mustafa Kemal and Enver never developed a personal relationship. More importantly, in the wake of the July revolution, Enver's status as one of the leaders of the revolt accelerated his career within both the imperial army and the CUP.

Reflecting back on the first days of the revolution, Mustafa Kemal later asserted that he soon fell out of favor with the CUP's central committee. In 1922, he stated that he initially viewed the CUP's motivations for revolution in a "pure and disinterested" light.[10] However, with increased internal jockeying for power within the committee, and the prospect of the Ottoman army taking greater power appearing more likely, he progressively harbored more apprehension toward his comrades. His early hostility toward the CUP's long-term plans, Atatürk later claimed, led the committee's leadership to marginalize him politically within the group's operations. Historians, in hindsight, dispute this rendering of his first years as a member of the post-revolutionary order. More than anything, Mustafa Kemal's retelling of his initial relationship with his fellow Young Turks served as a means to foreshadow his later repudiation of the CUP and justify his emergence as a man apart from his peers.

Weeks after the re-establishment of the constitution, the CUP's central committee dispatched Mustafa Kemal from Salonika with an important diplomatic task. In September 1908, he arrived in Libya, the empire's last province in North Africa. There he met with a series of prominent local political leaders who represented both the state bureaucracy and the region's tribal interests. The object of his mission was to reassure them that the revolution would not result in Abdülhamid II's dethronement and that the forthcoming parliamentary regime would lead to better governance and greater security. Accounts of the reactions Mustafa Kemal received during this trip appear to differ. Some biographers pose that he was successful in assuaging the fears of local Libyan political leaders who worried that the CUP intended to assume control over the empire at large. Mustafa Kemal impressed upon representatives in both Benghazi and Tripoli that this would not be the case, a pledge that resulted in the release of several CUP representatives taken captive before his arrival. Still, other accounts stress residual apprehensions toward the Young Turks and their future political designs. According to a British diplomat present at one meeting in Benghazi, notables who greeted Mustafa Kemal demanded that he produce credentials demonstrating that he spoke on the behalf of the sultan. When he admitted that he possessed no such document, the notables dissolved the meeting, claiming that the "Arabs recognize three Authorities, viz. God, the Prophet and the Sultan or Khalif [caliph]."[11]

Regardless of whether or not his mission to Libya should be counted as a success, the misgivings Mustafa Kemal encountered that fall were typical of the political mood many local leaders harbored in the months that followed the Young Turk Revolution. The initial euphoria that welcomed the restoration of the 1876 constitution in many parts of the empire soon subsided as some began to contemplate the meaning and ramifications of Abdülhamid II's decision. Despite the domineering reputation he had cultivated over the course of his rule, the sultan remained the object of personal and political devotion to many in the capital and the provinces. Abdülhamid II, through a series of overtures, specifically fostered closer ties with notables from the empire's Arabic-speaking territories. Through such acts as the construction of the Hijaz railway, which linked Istanbul to the holy cities of Mecca and Medina, he staked greater claim to the title of caliph, or ecumenical leader, of all Sunni Muslims, and imbued the Ottoman monarchy with greater authority and legitimacy. Under the auspices of Abdülhamid II's Islamist approach toward governance, notables from provinces with large Muslim populations, particularly in Albanian and Arabic-speaking regions, attained great favors and privileges from the palace. Conversely, the sultan's conciliatory policies toward the empire's Muslims served to alienate many Christians living in both the towns and the countryside.

The Young Turk Revolution, it appeared to many, complicated Abdülhamid II's future tenure as ruler of the empire. If a constitution placed constraints upon the sultan's ability to govern the state, what policies would result in turn? Would the restored constitution, for example, allow provincial notables to maintain the political status they had achieved under the sultan's patronage? Would the parliament, as a body drawn from every corner of the empire, address the concerns of both Muslim and Christian citizens as the Young Turk revolutionaries promised? More pointedly, what role would the CUP play in the crafting of this new liberal order? From the contemporary perspective of observers and commentators speaking or writing from the vantage point of late 1908 or early 1909, there was no general consensus as to how events would unfold with the convening of a new parliament. Mustafa Kemal, despite later voicing some trepidation toward the CUP's role in political affairs, did not appear to have posed any answers to these questions either.

The future involvement of the Ottoman sultan in parliamentary affairs was an issue that was in part resolved during the first half of 1909. On April 13, four months after the first session of the empire's elected assembly, a coalition of conservative and monarchist forces staged a coup against parliament, driving many key CUP figures in the capital into hiding. The CUP's central committee, from their main base in Salonika, responded quickly to the blow and rallied an army of loyal soldiers to liberate the capital from the coup plotters. Having returned from Libya a few months in advance, Mustafa Kemal was among the staff officers to join the Young Turk column on its march toward Istanbul. Two days of street battles ensued following the arrival of CUP forces to the city on April 24. When the fighting concluded, the principle coup plotters were tried, convicted, and executed for treason.

The parliament, once again restored by the CUP, voted unanimously to depose Abdülhamid II and replaced him with his younger, and more politically pliable, brother Mehmet V. Thereafter, no sultan would challenge the legal authority of the constitution, or the CUP, until the empire had all but completely collapsed.

Parliament's survival prompted the CUP to withdraw as an armed, overt force in Ottoman politics. Mustafa Kemal, for example, returned to his duties in Salonika while Enver, who had helped lead the suppression of the countercoup of 1909, took a posting in Berlin as a military attaché. The committee's influence, however, did not recede with the disbanding of the army that seized Istanbul in the spring of 1909. Parliamentary elections in the fall of 1908 allowed the committee to reinvent itself from a clandestine organization into a legal political party, a party which came to dominate the first session of the imperial assembly. Even with its success in the 1908 revolution, the central committee did not abandon its covert tendencies. The central committee continued to preside in secret over its growing ranks over the following years. By the outbreak of World War I in 1914, cells of furtive CUP loyalists were found at every level of the Ottoman military and bureaucracy. Through its legislative influence, coupled with the presence of large numbers of followers within the imperial administration, the committee became a veritable state within a state.

Mustafa Kemal's participation in the CUP's march on the capital did not result in an immediate rise in political authority within the committee's inner circle. Later in 1909, he did participate in a conference of CUP members held in Salonika. Slated as a representative from Libya, he voiced his opposition to the military's involvement in politics, a proposal that eventually was formally adopted, but not necessarily followed, by the party.

In the summer of 1910, he journeyed to France as a member of a military delegation sent to observe French army maneuvers. Only a few references to this trip are found within contemporary sources, even though it corresponded to Mustafa Kemal's first visit to Western Europe. After his brief stay in France, he returned to Salonika to resume his duties as a staff officer. Among his responsibilities that year was to participate in the suppression of a revolt in the predominantly Albanian-speaking provinces of Kosova and İşkodra in the western Balkans. The rebellion, which first broke out in the spring, was sparked by an order to impose greater import duties on products arriving into the region. This and other displays of greater government interference in the provinces ignited the fury of many Albanians who earlier had supported the Young Turk Revolution. While many of those who rose up that spring in Kosova had declared that the Young Turks had "broken their solemn agreement," Mustafa Kemal conversely came to perceive the rebels as traitors and reactionaries.[12] In speaking with a German officer who congratulated him on the success of the army's offensive against the rebels, he declared the empire's soldiers had defended "the country from foreign aggression" and freed "the nation from fanaticism and intellectual slavery."[13]

This statement, as well as others from this period of his life, suggests that Mustafa Kemal agreed with one important element of the CUP's governing leaders. The empire, in order to stave off insurrection, invasion, and collapse, had to be centrally governed. The CUP, in concurrence with seminal Ottoman reformers of the nineteenth century, was steadfast in their conviction that provincial autonomy, let alone local resistance (armed or otherwise), had to be quashed. The lessons of the previous century, in the minds of CUP loyalists, dictated that loose or decentralized governance gave credence to local strongmen or dissident communities to rise in rebellion and separate from the empire. The building of a strong state, with Istanbul as its sole political center, was the only possible defense against the threat of foreign political and economic influence. Thus, as in the case of the Albanian revolts, suppressing local opposition to state centralization was not strictly an act of law enforcement. It embodied a preemptive strike against the potential disillusion of Ottoman authority within the empire's borders.

The statism found in Mustafa Kemal's reply to the German officer was testament to his strong convictions as an Ottoman nationalist. At every level of his military education, a wide body of books, instructors, and classmates undoubtedly inculcated him with a deep attachment to the empire and its history. What is unclear at this point in his life is what it meant exactly to be an Ottoman citizen and a soldier in the imperial army. The precise meaning of Ottoman national identity varied widely among the empire's diverse population. Moreover, how state functionaries and representatives (including the sultan) had defined the concept of the Ottoman nation had evolved immensely over the century preceding Mustafa Kemal's entrance into state service. Nominally speaking, the CUP maintained after the revolution that the empire and its government continued to represent the interests and aspirations of all its subjects, irrespective of one's language or religious confession. Muslims, Christians, and Jews (as well individuals from a variety of ethnic and linguistic backgrounds) did identify themselves with the Young Turk cause and continued to serve in the imperial administration in the postrevolutionary era. Even such groups as the Dashnaktsutiun, a prominent Armenian nationalist organization that previously engaged in violent attacks against the Ottoman government, forged a tenuous working relationship with the CUP in the aftermath of 1908.

Nevertheless, despite these commitments to a pluralistic view of the empire and its politics, many Muslims within the ranks of the CUP had cultivated a strong sense of resentment and distrust toward non-Muslims and other minorities even after the Young Turk Revolution. A number of incidents that had taken place over the quarter of a century preceding the CUP's rise to power, such as the Dashnaktsutiun's bombing of the central Ottoman Bank in 1896, Greece's seizure of the island of Crete in 1908, and the generalized pattern of *çete* violence in Macedonia, verified, in the minds of many Muslims, a general propensity toward disloyalty and nonconformity among Ottoman Christians. In the eyes of many Young Turks, the uprisings in Kosova in 1910, as well as the outbreak of revolt in the distant province of Yemen in 1905, tainted the calls of many Albanians and Arabs for greater amounts

of political and cultural autonomy from the Ottoman state. For
Mustafa Kemal and others within the CUP, it seemed clear that
many Muslims within the empire did not share the same devotion to the Ottoman nation they served.

In the years following the Young Turk Revolution, debates
over the genuine character and content of the Ottoman nation
raged within CUP circles. Many of those who had been educated
and trained under the reign of Abdülhamid II held that Muslims,
regardless of the language they spoke or culture they possessed,
comprised the core of the Ottoman state. This definition of the
loyal Ottoman nation was fitting for many within the CUP
who were raised by Albanian, Bosnian, Arab, Kurdish, or North
Caucasian families; they, despite their adherence to provincial
customs and culture, served the empire without exception or
hesitation. While a majority of Muslim members of the CUP may
have adhered to this notion of Ottoman nationalism, an unknown
number of Young Turks perceived the core of the Ottoman nation
in more finite and ethnically exclusive terms. Muslim Turks, according to this subset of the CUP, embodied the true cultural
spirit and demographic heart of the empire. Supporters of this
consensus centered on a small clique of writers and intellectuals
based in Mustafa Kemal's hometown of Salonika. The chief advocate of this "Turkist" view of Ottoman nationalism was a young
intellectual of mixed Kurdish-Turkish descent by the name of
Ziya Gökalp. According to Gökalp, the Turks were a people whose
roots stretched through the Balkans, Anatolia, the Caucasus, and
Central Asia. Bound by history, language, and culture, the empire's future rested squarely in the hands of Turks who adhered to
strictly secular and modernist views of Islam. While Islam did
provide a glue that bound the nation together, Gökalp held that
Turkish culture had a historic and intrinsically moderating effect
upon the religion; Arabs and Iranians, who remained in his opinion more fervently attached to the theological contours of Islam,
would remain thusly more backward and "oriental" than their
Turkish neighbors.

PROCLAMATION DE LA CONSTITUTION OTTOMANE
le 11/24 Juillet 1908
La foule arrivant devant le Konak pour entendre la proclamation
de la Constitution par l'inspecteur général Hilmi Pacha

A REVOLUTION WITH HIGH ASPIRATIONS. *Demonstrators celebrating the restoration of the constitution in 1908 in Manastır.*

It is not clear if, or to what extent, Mustafa Kemal personally knew Ziya Gökalp. Although he certainly traveled in similar social circles as Gökalp and his consortium of like-minded intellectuals (often referred to as the "Young Writers"), there is no concrete evidence from this period that suggests to what degree Mustafa adhered to or was influenced by Turkist writings or opinions at this point in his life. Contemporary sources are equally as silent on his views on Islam and its relationship with the Ottoman nation. Through the prism of his later struggles and achievement, Atatürk did profess an affinity toward both the Muslim character of the Ottoman nation-state, as well as the specifically Turkish nature of the empire. Yet it is unclear whether or not these claims, which were mostly made in the years after World War I, reflected beliefs he held as an officer in the Balkans. Further complicating our understanding of how Mustafa Kemal's views evolved as a young man are the general inconsistencies found among Turkist and Islamist thinkers and advocates during the prewar era. Proponents of Ottoman Muslim nationalism at times differed on the degree to which Islam's tenants and precepts should shape state governance and reform. Turkism was equally beset by contradictions and ambiguity. Turkishness, in the minds of many Ottoman Muslims, was not defined by biological or purely ethnic traits. The Turkish language was long the lingua franca of the empire. For both Muslims and non-Muslims, speaking Turkish was a marker of refinement and civility associated with education and urban living. In a state as diverse as the Ottoman Empire, mixed marriages and complex family trees were common (as seen in the case of both Mustafa Kemal and Ziya Gökalp). In many places in the Ottoman Empire, the term "Turk" was commonly used synonymously for Muslims regardless of their ethnic background (likewise, the Ottoman Empire and Turkey were names that were used interchangeably by people both inside and outside of the state's borders for centuries). Considering all of the complexities that defined identity in the late Ottoman Empire, one can only speculate as to how Mustafa Kemal navigated the incongruities and debates that affected Ottoman nationalist discourse during his youth. Evidence from the latter stages of his life suggest that his opinions and convictions continued to evolve as political conditions in the empire changed after the onset of World War I.

Mustafa Kemal's fealty to the state and the army was put to the test in September 1911. That fall, Italy declared war upon Istanbul and invaded the province of Libya. Rome's desire to seize the empire's last territorial holdings in North Africa followed in the footsteps of other European states that had successfully seized land and other concessions from the Ottoman sultan. By that point in his life, a series of European interventions had passed that had resulted in the de facto or de jure loss of the territories of Cyprus, Bulgaria, Bosnia, Tunisia, and Egypt. In the absence of direct imperial response, he and other CUP officers volunteered to lead a guerrilla campaign to turn back the Italian invasion. Along with three companions, he slipped into Libya in disguise and joined a camp of other Ottoman officers and irregulars who had mustered from other parts of the empire. The base, which was located outside of the Italian beachhead at Darna in the eastern part of modern Libya, was placed under the command of Enver, who had left his post in Berlin earlier to join the fight. By that point in time, the former hero of the Young Turk Revolution had established himself as a principal figure within the CUP. His status as an individual of significant political weight was particularly furthered when the sultan's niece accepted his proposal for marriage. With close ties to both the palace and the CUP's central committee, Enver was additionally tasked with securing the loyalties of local notables in Libya. Their shared desire to evict the Italians from Libya prevented Mustafa Kemal from clashing with Enver over the conduct of the campaign. Nonetheless, the acrimony that developed between the two officers was to such an extent that it attracted the attention of officers in Istanbul.

His training in the Harbiye, coupled with his experiences in the field in Macedonia, clearly prepared Mustafa Kemal for his duties in the Libya campaign. As the commander of a detachment comprising scores of regular officers and thousands of local fighters, he successfully held off repeated Italian attempts to break out of their beachhead at Darna. The experience of command, as seen in one letter he posted from the front, filled him at first with admiration and pride for those who served with him. The sight of officers and men from Libya and outside of the province restored his faith in the survival of the empire since the fatherland had so many children "willing to sacrifice their safety and happiness for those in the country and the nation."[14] Despite the best efforts of Enver, Mustafa Kemal, and other CUP volunteers, Istanbul's ability to defend and retain Libya proved fleeting. With the outbreak of a general war in the Balkans in October 1912, most regular officers, including Mustafa Kemal, gradually evacuated from the front and returned home. Fighting between Italian and local forces continued well after the formal withdrawal of Ottoman troops, leading to over thirty years of colonial rule in Libya.

Mustafa Kemal's service as a wartime field commander did not end with his departure from Libya. Much of his life over the next twelve years was spent in combat on the frontlines. His departure from Libya in October 1912 stands as an important juncture in his life for other reasons. Thereafter, his relationship with Enver and others within CUP grew more heated and disagreeable. Despite these tensions, he did continue to rise through the ranks of the Ottoman army and served notably on various fronts in the Balkans and during World War I. Most important, the end of his service in Libya and the onset of the Balkan Wars marked a personal turn in Mustafa Kemal's development and maturation. With the fall of Salonika in November 1912, he, along within many of the CUP's early followers, became a refugee in his own land.

It is difficult to interpret Mustafa Kemal's life between 1880 and 1911 without resorting to the comments and recollections he and others put forward later in life. By the time he became president, Atatürk and his closest associates had already begun to describe and explain his youth through the filter of his ensuing fame. For this reason, it may not be possible for us to understand his true thoughts and experiences before his rise to national and international prominence. The sources that are available, however, do allow us to contextualize and appreciate several key elements of his early character and outlook.

Mustafa Kemal represented an emerging Muslim middle class that had begun to take shape by the late nineteenth century. This middle class, which was found predominantly in the major cities of the Ottoman Empire, possessed many of the tastes and intellectual interests that were typical of middle-class culture in Europe and elsewhere during this period of time. He was undoubtedly secular in his views on religion and favored many of the modernist intellectual trends of the era. Strong nationalist convictions and a desire for upward mobility compelled him, as well as many other young Muslim men, to choose a life in the military. His graduation from the Ottoman Military Academy in Istanbul stands as a testament to both his acumen as a student and his status as an emerging member of the imperial elite.

Mustafa Kemal grew up at a time when the social fabric of the empire was beginning to fray and dissolve in many corners of the realm. As an officer stationed in Macedonia, Syria, and Libya, he witnessed firsthand the violent repercussions of the empire's failing fortunes. In this era of crisis, he was drawn to the politics of dissent that eventually inspired the overthrow of the sitting sultan, Abdülhamid II. His inclusion into the ranks of the CUP assured him a place in the administration of the last governing body of the Ottoman Empire. At this stage in his life, however, Mustafa Kemal was by no means a preeminent player in the CUP. He remained a vocal, but still relatively minor, CUP functionary well into World War I.

It is more difficult to pinpoint Mustafa Kemal's ideological leanings by the time he left Libya in 1911. As an officer who helped bring the CUP to power in 1908, he clearly supported the party's commitment to state centralization and reform. His experiences in the field further conditioned him as a proponent of Ottoman nationalism. Yet, from his position as a middle-ranking staff officer, it is unclear how he perceived the future of the Ottoman nation at the outbreak of the Balkan Wars. One can only assume that he was a party to discussions and debates in CUP circles in Salonika and Istanbul on the Muslim and Turkish character of the nation. While Mustafa Kemal may not have taken a definitive stand on these issues in the years preceding World War I, such debates clearly had an effect upon the policies he later imposed as president of the Republic of Turkey.

Mustafa Kemal's youth in Salonika and Istanbul also impacted the kind of state he helped to craft out of the embers of the Ottoman Empire. His aspirations to build a Turkey that "faced West" and embodied the modern, bourgeois trends of Europe were first informed by his early life in the Ottoman Balkans. While not serving as the explicit model for the republic's development, the sophistication of Salonika's cafés, theaters, and markets provided an early framework with which Atatürk and other Turkish reformers set out to transform Anatolia into the heartland of a modern state. Mustafa Kemal never returned to the city of his birth, but it did not completely stray from his thoughts as he grew older. At his dinner table, the aging Young Turk continued to delight in the Macedonian folk songs he first heard as a young man.

CHAPTER 2

| ATATÜRK AS A SOLDIER, |
1912–1918

MUSTAFA KEMAL RETURNED TO THE CAPITAL from the Libyan front
in November 1912. The intervening weeks between his final days
outside of Darna and his arrival to Istanbul comprised, up until
that point, the most devastating and traumatizing period in
the history of the Ottoman state. On October 8, the armies of
Montenegro, Serbia, Greece, and Bulgaria began a rapid, coordinated offensive across the empire's Macedonian frontier. Early
defeats compounded the Ottoman army's inability to reinforce
its flagging forces. Despite decades of reform and investment,
the empire's army desperately gave ground on multiple fronts.
Advancing Greek, Bulgarian, and Serb troops, after dispatching the
Ottoman army and putting it to flight, massacred large numbers
of Muslim civilians as they progressed deeper into the Macedonian
and Thracian countryside. While Ottoman forces held firm against
the Balkan League attacks in the Albanian highlands, troops defending Istanbul were forced to retreat eastward, exposing the
city of Edirne, once the imperial capital, to a shattering five-month-
long siege. Attempts at reaching an armistice between December
and January 1913 did not prevent the fall of Edirne or other major
Ottoman citadels.

A fragile peace between the Ottoman Empire and the Balkan
League was secured with the signing of the Treaty of London at

the end of May 1913. Istanbul paid an unconscionable price in seeking an end to the war. All of Ottoman Macedonia and much of Thrace were ceded to Greece, Serbia, and Bulgaria. With much of the empire's Albanian-speaking territory cut off from the capital, Albanian nationalists seized upon this moment of crisis to declare a separate, independent Albanian state with Tirana as its capital.

Mustafa Kemal's delayed return from North Africa prevented him from playing a part in the empire's defeat in Macedonia. Greek troops entered his native Salonika around the same time of his arrival to the capital in early November. Before a party of friends seated in an Istanbul café, his mood following the loss of his hometown was angry and morose. "How could you do this?" he posed to his comrades. "How could you surrender that beautiful Salonika to the enemy? How could you sell it so cheaply?"[1] Mustafa Kemal's lamentation touched upon two deeply embedded and consequential themes that defined his character as he matured into a man and a senior officer in the service of the empire. The declaration, on the one hand, reflected the unquestioned sense of loss and humiliation he experienced as a result of the Ottoman state's losses on the battlefield. One can only imagine that Salonika's surrender and his displacement from his hometown amplified and personalized the pain and disgrace caused by the empire's deteriorating condition. The hurt incurred over the fall of the Ottoman Balkans undoubtedly continued to plague him as the empire lurched from one war to the next over the following decade.

On the other hand, it is clear from his words that he did not blame the invading Greeks solely for Salonika's capitulation. The Ottoman military's high command bore some responsibility for this calamity as well. This attack upon his superiors over the fall of Salonika echoed past feuds with Enver and other powerful figures in the Committee of Union and Progress (CUP) over the organization's political and military conduct. Mustafa Kemal's quarrelsome disposition toward those who outranked him reflected more than just his personal frustration with the management of the state in this moment of crisis. It also foreshadowed his growing political ambitions at the expense of those already in power.

The six years separating the outbreak of the Balkan Wars and Istanbul's surrender in World War I were indeed a dark time for Mustafa Kemal. As the commander of ever-larger contingents of men and material on multiple fronts, he bore witness to the empire's collapse and the complete degradation of the army he had committed to serve since his youth. The depredations he observed firsthand extended into society through his tours of villages and towns racked by violence, starvation, and lawlessness. Yet for all of the hardships he experienced during these years, Mustafa Kemal's charisma, sacrifice, and heroism as a commander precipitated a dramatic rise in his personal stature within the ranks of the Ottoman state. It was during this period that he attained the rank of *Pasha*, an honorific title reserved for the highest ranking generals and statesmen in the empire. His exploits on the battlefield secured him a reputation that insulated him from the political infighting in Istanbul and the popular rage that engulfed the countryside following the empire's capitulation in 1918. With World War I's conclusion, the political fortunes of many of his enemies began to wane, allowing Mustafa Kemal an opportunity to attain the power and authority he had long sought for himself.

Only a few days passed between his return to Istanbul and his appointment to a posting on the frontlines. His new duties as a staff officer took him to the Gallipoli Peninsula on the banks of the Dardanelles Straits, the main waterway connecting the Sea of Marmara with the Aegean. Mustafa Kemal's posting to the region's main headquarters in Bolayır placed him in close proximity to the capital, which at the time was in a general state of upheaval. CUP control over the parliament and governing cabinet had weakened during his stint as a field commander in Libya. The growing strength of an opposition party called the Liberal Entente led the CUP's central committee to undertake more direct and illicit means to ensure its hold on power (steps that included gerrymandering electoral districts and intimidating opposition candidates and voters). Events came to a head in January 1913 when the sitting GRAND VIZIR, the head of the constitutional government, began to entertain a Bulgarian peace overture that would have allowed for the cessation of Edirne. Indignant at the thought of surrendering a city still in Ottoman hands, a cabal of junior officers led by Enver struck against the cabinet. On January 23, Enver headed a large party of supporters into the Sublime Porte, the empire's main bureaucratic offices, and forced the GRAND VIZIR to resign at gunpoint.

The coup marked a definitive turning point in both the evolution of the CUP and signaled a dramatic change in how the empire would be managed until the conclusion of World War I. Enver's attack upon the Sublime Porte paved the way for the formation of a CUP government that would stand unopposed in executing policies it deemed fit for the good of the nation. The coup rendered the parliament an impotent and pliant tool for the CUP's central committee, which assumed supreme power in defining and dictating the empire's goals and designs. However, the events of January 1913 did not lead to greater harmony within the CUP as a party or a governing branch of the Ottoman state. Factionalist struggles hampered relations within the CUP's ranks as strong personalities and differences of opinion over political and military affairs increased over time. Mustafa Kemal, for example, allied himself strongly with the interests and activities of Ahmet Cemal Pasha, a senior CUP officer and rival of Enver.

The change in government had a direct effect upon Mustafa Kemal's duties on the Bolayır front. In early February, a combination of land and amphibious forces attacked Bulgarian positions along the Gallipoli front. Ottoman troops initially drove the Bulgarians back, but the assault ultimately failed due to stiff opposition and the late arrival of the amphibious units. Tempers flared within the army's high command following the Ottoman defeat outside of Bolayır. Mustafa and Ali Fethi Okyar, his friend and commanding officer, threatened to resign from their posts when the leader of the amphibious attack, Fahri Pasha, was ordered to take charge of the Bolayır sector. In response to this quarrel within the Ottoman headquarters at Bolayır, the new GRAND VIZIR personally visited the front and relieved Fahri of command. Fahri's dismissal only partially resolved the tensions on the Gallipoli front. In a separate memorandum, Ali Fethi and Mustafa lobbied the GRAND VIZIR for the complete transfer of their units to the center of the Ottoman lines at Çatalca in the hopes of executing an attack that would liberate Edirne from Bulgarian control. Moreover, the two advocated that Enver, who had been transferred to Istanbul to take charge of the Ottoman army's general staff, also be relieved of his duties. In the end, Mustafa Kemal remained at his post in Bolayır while Enver, along with troops from the Galipolli front, was transferred to Çatalca in anticipation of a large offensive against the Bulgarian center. Fortunately for the Ottomans, the collapse of the Balkan League, and the outbreak of the Second Balkan War in June 1913, provided a pretext for this planned liberation of Edirne. With the Bulgarians occupied on other fronts, Ottoman forces advanced westward across Thrace and seized Edirne on July 22. Enver personally and ceremoniously placed himself at the head of the first column of men entering the city, an act that further solidified his reputation as a military commander and national hero.

Mustafa Kemal's participation in the Balkan Wars contrasts sharply with the fame and stature Enver achieved by the war's end. As a result of his dispute with senior officers in Istanbul, he hardened his reputation as a fractious figure within the officer corps' upper ranks. While he did participate in the offensive that led to the recapture of Edirne and eastern Thrace, Kemal still elicited little distinction as a battlefield commander. Speaking years later in an interview with a Turkish newspaper, Atatürk made a point of demeaning Enver's role in the conflict, stating that his seizure of Edirne "could not be counted an active command since it had been undertaken against a Bulgarian army which had ceased to exist after its defeat by Serbs, Greeks and Romanians."[2]

Whether deserved or not, Enver's participation in the Edirne campaign launched him into positions of greater power while Mustafa Kemal remained a promising but politically marginal officer.

His retention within the Ottoman army, despite his displays of insubordination at Bolayır, does suggest, however, that Mustafa Kemal remained an individual of some political weight within the army and the CUP. Historians have come to interpret the controversies involving his Balkan War disputes as an indication that he remained a valued, and perhaps protected, figure within an increasingly politicized Ottoman military. Moreover, the fact that a junior officer could criticize his superiors and be retained without receiving any obvious penalties, some have posed, was generally symbolic of the tortured state of the CUP's manner of governance during this period of profound crisis.

The conclusion of the Second Balkan War allowed Mustafa Kemal to enjoy a brief respite from the soldiering that had preoccupied him over the previous years. In October 1913, he followed his friend and comrade Ali Fethi to Bulgaria, where he had been appointed to serve as the Ottoman Ambassador. As Fethi's attaché, his duties were light compared to the service he previously rendered in Thrace and Libya. During his fourteen-month stay in Sofia, some of Atatürk's biographers have suggested that he drew a certain amount of inspiration from his experiences intermingling with various levels of Bulgarian society. While living in Sofia, he made the acquaintance of many of Bulgaria's presiding military and civilian elite (including the reigning king, Ferdinand). His exposure to Sofia's political elite, which openly reveled in the Western norms of the era, may have had an effect upon his future views on reform and modernization while president of the Republic of Turkey. Bulgaria, after all, had been a key part of the Ottoman Empire's Balkan holdings. Yet, after only a few decades of independence, aspects of the Bulgarian state and society had assumed many of the attributes of a modern country under the influence of a wide series of reforms. Bulgaria's transformation from an imperial province into a seemingly modern nation-state also impacted the country's Muslim minority (which made up a considerable percentage of the young state's overall population). His responsibilities as a representative of the Ottoman government brought him into contact with Turkish-speaking Muslims who outwardly appeared to conform to the manners and tastes of contemporary Europe. For example, he befriended and regularly socialized with one of Bulgaria's Muslim members of parliament, Şakir Zümre, a man who later became an active supporter of the Kemalist cause during the Turkish War of Independence.

Ali Fethi did not completely share in Mustafa Kemal's admiration of Bulgarian society or its treatment of the country's Muslim minority. For Fethi, Bulgaria's departure from the empire served as a bitter lesson to the Ottoman Empire. The establishment of this separate state not only humiliated the once proud empire but left millions of former Ottoman citizens (particularly Muslims) "abandoned to their fate."[3] During the period in which both Mustafa Kemal and Ali Fethi worked in the Ottoman Embassy in Sofia, thousands of Bulgarian Muslims fled their homes in order to escape violent acts of retribution and other oppressive governmental policies following the Balkan Wars. Refugees escaping from Bulgaria during this period joined tens of thousands of other Muslims from Greece and Serbia who sought refuge in the Ottoman Empire. By the time the Turkish Republic was established in 1923, government census takers would estimate that over 500,000 Muslims had absconded from the Balkans and taken up residence in Anatolia. Counted among this great wave of refugees was Mustafa Kemal's mother, who came to reside in Istanbul after the fall of Salonika in November 1912. Atatürk makes no reference to his feelings or views toward the plight of his family or refugees during this period in his life. Despite his silence on this issue, events later in his life leave little doubt that questions surrounding the future of Muslims living in the Balkans weighed heavily upon his mind.

Biographers have also tended to highlight Mustafa Kemal's interlude in Sofia as an important chapter in his desire to court a bride. After his return to Istanbul in 1913, he struck up a friendship with a young woman named Corrine, the widow of a friend and comrade who died in the Balkan Wars. Corrine, who was the daughter of an Italian doctor living in Istanbul, maintained contact with Mustafa during his stay in Bulgaria. The letters he sent to her often mentioned his affection for her, although they do not suggest that he intended to pursue her hand in marriage. In his letters, he mentions socializing with other single women who, like Corrine, were from Western Europe and possessed European sensibilities and tastes. While none of the female acquaintances he met in Bulgaria became his wife, scholars have often portrayed his interest in Western (or Westernized) women at this stage of his life as evidence of his support for women's emancipation. The fact that he, as a young man, did not seek a more traditional or conservative woman as a friend or spouse suggests that Mustafa Kemal championed secular or progressive policies and issues affecting women well before he became president of the Turkish Republic in 1923.

During his first year in Sofia, Istanbul continued to struggle with the political consequences of the Balkan Wars. Even after the seizure of Edirne, the loss of Macedonia and Albania, as well as the displacement of hundreds of thousands of Muslim citizens, represented more than a daunting humanitarian and strategic crisis. The war, in the eyes of many within the CUP-controlled government, sullied the honor and threatened the integrity of the Ottoman state and its military. The prospect of further conflict with Greece, as well as suspicions toward the loyalties of Orthodox Christians still residing in the empire, raised tensions even further within both the capital and the provinces. In this climate of fear, humiliation, and warmongering, Enver (who was awarded the rank of *Pasha* after his dramatic entrance into Edirne) became the minister of war. During the first half of 1914, Enver formed a troika government alongside two other longstanding CUP officials, Talat Pasha, minister of the interior, and Ahmed Cemal Pasha, then minister of the navy. Together, this triumvirate regime sought to stir popular nationalist passions as well as fortify and prepare the bureaucracy and military for the eventual armed conflicts to follow. As the Ottoman foreign ministry sought to forge alliances with conflicting members of Europe's Great Powers, Enver purged the army of hundreds of officers deemed too old or unfit for command in future wars. Government officials increasingly advocated the construction of a national economy, one that emphasized and favored local (particularly Muslim) entrepreneurs and traders at the expense of Westerners and native Christians. An unofficial national boycott of Orthodox Christian businesses (a violent campaign that forced tens of thousands to flee to Greece) complimented the CUP government's endorsement of an economy in which entrepreneurial Muslims held greater power and influence. By the summer of 1914, official statements, as well as the private musings of CUP officials, became ever more explicit that Ottoman Muslims were the heart and soul of the Ottoman nation and that the Ottoman nation would soon be called upon to fight for its survival.

Archduke Franz Ferdinand's assassination in Sarajevo in June 1914 fulfilled the CUP's bellicose prophecies and expectations. Within two weeks of Austria-Hungary's declaration of war upon Serbia, the Ottoman Empire finalized an alliance with Germany, bringing Istanbul onto the side of the Central Powers. A number of factors influenced the Ottoman decision to side with Berlin and eventually enter World War I. A broad consensus prevailed within the CUP that the outbreak of a generalized war within Europe would impact the Ottoman Empire. One way or another, such a conflict threatened the very existence of the state, leaving Istanbul no choice but to seek a military alliance with one of the two grand European alliances. The potent military capabilities of Germany's large, sophisticated army only partially explains Istanbul's choice to align the Ottoman state with the Central Powers. Germany, unlike Britain, France, or Russia, had never demanded territory from the empire and professed no obvious or outward irredentist designs on the eastern Mediterranean. In the short term, Berlin's relationship with the Ottoman Empire would allow Istanbul to exercise greater amounts of independence and self-determination in the event of an invasion by members of the Entente. More important, war, in the eyes of the CUP, provided a means to unify and mobilize popular support for the government in the time of crisis and humiliation following the Balkan Wars. Success on the battlefield, many hoped, would allow Istanbul to recoup some of the territorial losses that the Ottomans had suffered in both the Balkans and the Caucasus. With these aims in mind, the Ottomans declared war upon Russia, France, and Great Britain on November 10, 1914.

Mustafa Kemal did not share in the government's enthusiasm for war. His writings from this period suggest that he was pessimistic in his evaluation of the Ottoman alliance with Germany. From his perspective in Sofia, the empire's objectives in entering the war, as well as the possibility that Germany could simultaneously defeat both France and Russia, remained uncertain. His apprehensions, however, did not prevent him from seeking a return to active duty. In January 1915, the Ministry of War approved his removal from the Ottoman embassy in Sofia. After passing through Istanbul, Mustafa Kemal assumed command of the Ottoman Nineteenth Division located in the town of Tekirdağ. Located within a day's journey of the Dardanelles Straits, he once again found himself in command of troops tasked with defending this vital waterway to the Aegean Sea. Overall command of the strait's defenses fell to Liman von Saunders, a German field marshal sent by Berlin to advise the Ottoman military. Relations between Mustafa and von Saunders were purportedly tense from the start. Despite the ill feelings he may have harbored toward his German superior (as well as Enver and the Ministry of War for appointing him to command the front), a combined British and French naval attack upon the straits in mid-February 1915 indicated a direct amphibious assault upon the Dardanelles was imminent, requiring all of those charged with defending the region to remain vigilant.

Other factors undoubtedly amplified Mustafa Kemal's fears of an allied assault within his sector. A month before his return to the regular military, Russian forces had inflicted a devastating defeat upon a large Ottoman army in the mountains outside the town of Sarıkamış in eastern Anatolia. The effects of the intensely cold winter and hostile environment further aggravated Ottoman losses as the Russian army pressed their advance westward. Attempts at an Ottoman offensive on the Sinai Peninsula in February 1915 equally failed to gain the initiative after British forces held firm in their defense of the Suez Canal. Further east in Ottoman Iraq, British troops advanced and seized the provincial capital of Basra in November 1914. Worse still, the German offensive against the French lines outside of Paris had stalled while Russian columns made gains against Austria-Hungary in Galicia. A second British and French naval assault on the straits in March 1915 was an indication of the confidence the Entente possessed in bringing the war to the Dardanelles. It was clear that should the Entente's forces pass the straits and enter the Sea Marmara, Ottoman land and naval forces would be helpless to prevent Istanbul from falling into enemy hands.

Sensing that a death blow could be struck, a fleet carrying an army made up of French and British regular and colonial troops moved into position on the outer banks of the Gallipoli Peninsula in mid-April 1915. On the morning of the April 25, the vanguard of the Allied assault waded onto shore along six separate beaches and slowly moved inland. The landing caught Liman von Saunders and the Ottoman high command by surprise despite the weeks they had to prepare the peninsula's defenses for a ground invasion. Confusion reigned within the headquarters of the Ottoman units stationed along the Gallipoli front as intelligence from the British beachheads along the western coast slowly seeped in. Outside of a small bay of water later called Anzac Cove (or Arıburunu in Turkish), contingents of Australian soldiers made steady progress that morning against the thinly held heights surrounding the sea. Mustafa Kemal, upon hearing of the landing later that

A COMMANDER AT THE FRONT. *Mustafa Kemal among his men in the trenches outside of Gallipoli.*

morning, drew up his division and marched them across the rough and hilly landscape in the direction of the advancing Australians. As he approached a rise within a few kilometers of the water, he encountered Ottoman soldiers fleeing from the front. With the Australians seemingly within minutes of seizing the heights commanding the center of the peninsula, Mustafa Kemal, without orders, commanded the men around him to prepare to attack. The troops that had already met the Australians earlier that morning protested that they were out of ammunition. Taking personal command of the Ottoman Fifty-Seventh Regiment, he then gave the order to fix bayonets. Atatürk later reflected upon this key moment and gave this rendition of the events that followed:

> To my mind there was a more important factor than this tactical situation—that was everybody hurled himself on the enemy to kill and to die. This was no ordinary attack. Everybody was eager to succeed or go forward with the determination to die. Here is the order which I gave verbally to the commanders: 'I don't order you to attack—I order you to die. In the time which passes until we die, other troops and commanders can take our place.'[4]

Upon his command, the men of the Fifty-Seventh Regiment swiftly marched in a line of battle toward the Australian positions on the hill before them. The bayonet charge stunned the Australians and sent them reeling as Mustafa Kemal and his men pushed on. By the end of the morning, the Fifty-Seventh Regiment's counterattack helped to secure two strategic hilltops, denying the allies a tactical advantage in their attempts to widen their foothold at the center of the Gallipoli Peninsula. Intense fighting continued to rage days after the initial landings. Despite securing five separate beaches on the morning of April 25, British imperial troops remained hemmed into their defensive positions in the face of stiff Ottoman opposition in the interior. British hopes for a swift victory dissipated within weeks as both sides dug in, transforming the peninsula into an intricate patchwork of trenches, bunkers, and redoubts.

At the sight of his auspicious victory (later renamed "Kemal's Place" or Kemalyeri), Mustafa Kemal was presented with the Distinguished Service Medal for his valorous leadership. His distinction as a tested frontline commander became more resolute as heavy fighting continued along his lines during the course of

May and June. On the night of June 29, he sent his division into battle against the Entente lines. While he later claimed that he received an order to push forward, his Nineteenth Division attacked the opposing trenches without coordinated support, resulting in heavy casualties and no territorial advantage. In early August, British forces redeployed further north of the Ottoman lines surrounding Anzac Cove. Once again, Mustafa Kemal was called upon to lead a counterattack aimed at retaking a key line of hills facing the sea. While personally commanding one bayonet charge, a piece of shrapnel struck his chest, smashing a watch in his breast pocket. His determination that day, in spite of his brush with death, earned him further admiration from von Sanders and his fellow officers. By the conclusion of the campaign, Mustafa Kemal's acts of valor and resolve earned him a promotion to the rank of colonel and still other fine distinctions, such as the German Iron Cross.

A bloody stalemate ensued on the peninsula between June and December 1915. Like the fighting in Flanders on the Western Front, Ottoman and Allied forces remained firmly entrenched along a maze of fortified lines. Artillery and sniper fire continued to claim lives through the fall of 1915 as both sides continued to dig in. The intensity of the Aegean summer sun inflicted even greater hardships upon the lives of soldiers on both sides of the fighting. Perhaps the greatest threat to the life and limb of Ottoman and Entente troops was the outbreak of disease. The inherently unsanitary conditions of life in the trenches and bunkers along the Gallipoli front produced outbreaks of dysentery, malaria, cholera, and lice. Writing to his friend Corrine in Istanbul, Mustafa Kemal described life for him and the soldiers as nothing short of hell. For the men, the prospect of either "victory for the faith or martyrdom" provided the only solace to the horrors they witnessed.[5] His letter to Corrine makes it clear that he did not take much comfort (or stock) in promises of paradise in the afterlife. Nevertheless, the human toll from combat and illness certainly conditioned his outlook on the war.

By the time British forces fully withdrew from the Gallipoli Peninsula in December 1915, an official Ottoman survey calculated that over 164,000 officers and men had been killed, wounded, or gone missing during the fighting. Another 21,000 Ottoman soldiers died from disease, while 64,000 were evacuated from the front due to illness. Entente casualties were equally heavy, with the British and French officially claiming over a quarter of million casualties.[6]

While his bravery and determination as a field officer did earn him the respect of Liman von Sanders and others in the Ottoman high command, Mustafa Kemal's reputation for obstinacy and combativeness toward his superiors continued to grow while stationed in Gallipoli. He repeatedly clashed with von Sanders on tactics and strategy in the face of the British offensive. On more than one occasion he sought the intercession of generals in Istanbul in the hopes of changing the conduct of the campaign on the peninsula. His efforts to circumvent the chain of command prompted visits by Enver and Talat, minister of the interior, to his headquarters. Despite the positive impact von Sanders and other German officers had upon the successful defense of the region, Mustafa Kemal bristled at the authority held by foreign officers within the ranks of the Ottoman Empire. His bitterness toward von Sanders deepened after the Allied offensive in August. After threatening to resign yet again from his command, a lull in the fighting allowed him to return to Istanbul on sick leave. During his recovery from illness, the British completed their evacuation from Gallipoli. The end of the Gallipoli campaign, coupled with his recuperation, provided Mustafa Kemal with a new opportunity to take command of Ottoman forces along a new front. In April 1916, he was promoted to the rank of brigadier general and was transferred east to the town of Diyarbakir where he assumed command of the Ottoman Sixteenth Corps.

His tenure as a corps commander on the eastern front coincided with the planning of a general campaign against Russian forces occupying much of Anatolia's eastern frontier. Over the course of 1915, the Tsar's armies had captured the key cities of Erzurum, Trabzon, Van, Harput, and Bitlis. Ottoman forces continued to suffer in the wake of the disaster at Sarıkamış and continued to cede ground into the spring of 1916. The flight of tens of thousands of civilians from the Russian front further compounded the dire military situation in eastern Anatolia. In August 1916, the Ottoman Second Army staged a general counterattack against the Russian frontlines. Mustafa Kemal's Sixteenth Corps acquitted itself well during the offensive, seizing the towns of Bitlis and Muş after fierce fighting. The arrival of Russian reinforcements, as well as the onset of an early snowfall, compelled Ottoman troops to cease their advance and withdraw from the hard-won town of Bitlis. Fortunately for Istanbul, the failure of the August campaign, which cost the Ottoman Second Army over 100,000 casualties, did not lead to further territorial losses in Anatolia. By the spring of 1917, the outbreak of revolution in St. Petersburg slowly began to sap the resolve and initiative of Russian army units stationed south of the Caucasus. As 1917 came to a close, the tide in eastern Anatolia turned in Istanbul's favor as thousands of Russian soldiers abruptly abandoned their lines and returned home.

Mustafa Kemal kept a diary during a portion of his deployment to Diyarbakir. Within these pages of his journal he reflected upon a wide range of issues pertaining to his experiences and intellectual interests. Much of his journal documents his day-to-day encounters with refugees, soldiers, officers, and local political leaders in the war-torn regions of Diyarbakir, Silvan, and Bitlis. In addition to touching upon his emerging views on military discipline and leadership, his diary often references the books he read in his spare time. Among the more interesting topics he meditated upon in this period were debates surrounding religion, love, and the status of women. In his off-hours, Mustafa read a treatise entitled "Is It Possible to Deny God?," a work that debated one's ability to reconcile natural science with religious dogma. In one passage, he agreed with the notion that Islamic scholars, like contemporary Western observers, sought a more critical and rational reading of religion (one that was separate from popular belief). However, how the Islamic clergy tended to portray their religion still "contained many puzzling secrets."[7] In hindsight, comments such as these infer Mustafa Kemal's maturation as an individual with modernist secular views toward Islam and society.

His secularist and progressive tendencies are further demonstrated in his comments upon women. According to one passage, Mustafa Kemal spent an evening with his aide-de-camp during which they discussed the need for governments to improve the lives of women. He specifically suggested to his junior officer that greater education for mothers, the banning of public veiling for Muslim women, and greater freedom for men and women to express their feelings and affections (which he cryptically alludes to as a "common life") were essential for the advancement of women.[8] Other books he read in his leisure time affirm his open views of love and relationships. While at the front he read Alphonse Daudet's novel *Sapho*, which recounts an illicit love affair between a young, naïve army officer and a more adventurous, unmarried woman. The story, which concludes with the main female character reforming her ways by settling down with a more proper spouse, evidently did not appeal to him. Considering his relationship with Corrine, with whom he continued to correspond during his time in Anatolia, one could speculate that the conservative morals of the novel did not correspond to his views of relationships between men and women.

Despite the breadth of issues that weighed upon his mind during his tour of service in Diyarbakir, two specific topics relevant to life and politics in southeastern Anatolia at this point in the war seemed to have escaped his interest. Beginning in May 1915, the regional Ottoman government of Diyarbakir, under orders from Istanbul, initiated a policy of deporting the region's native Armenian population. Istanbul's decision to undertake such a heavy-handed action against its own citizens was partially rooted in the Ottoman army's failures on the battlefield and the growing instability of Anatolia after the commencement of the conflict. Following the defeat at Sarıkamış, Russian forces advanced across Anatolia with the aid of expatriate Armenian nationalists. News of local Armenian support for the Russian invasion heightened government suspicions that dissident Armenian nationalists were planning to foment revolt in Anatolia in anticipation of the outbreak of war. While some local Armenians aided Russian gains in such places as Van in April 1915, it is clear that the CUP government had begun to contemplate a general "evacuation" of Armenian civilians from eastern Anatolia before Istanbul formally initiated the policy in April 1915. In the case of Diyarbakir, the appointment of a new CUP governor in February of that year resulted in mass arrests of Armenian notables and demands that the Christian population surrender any and all firearms. By the end of the summer, Ottoman officials had forcibly compelled most of Diyarbakir's Armenian population, including women, children, and elderly people, to abandon their homes and march in the direction of Mosul, several hundred miles away to the south. Large numbers of these deportees died as a result of exposure, hunger, and exhaustion. An equally large number of Diyarbakir's Armenians (as well as other eastern Christians from throughout Anatolia) died at the hands of Ottoman soldiers and irregulars who attacked defenseless villages and columns of refugees without provocation. In the wake of the deportations, Ottoman officials and local leaders remanded an untold fortune in movable property and land left behind by dead and banished Armenians. The CUP government eagerly amassed Armenians goods, property and capital as a means of promoting a "national economy" that primarily benefited Muslim investors, producers and cultivators. While Unionist leaders did not publicly advocate the total extermination of the empire's Armenian population, the government's mass appropriation of property was based upon the presumption that the deported would not return.

The deportations, and much of the ensuing violence, had largely ended by the time Mustafa Kemal took up residence in Diyarbakir. Save the presence of hundreds of homeless, destitute

INNOCENT VICTIMS OF WAR. *Both the fighting and the government's deportation policies inflicted hundreds of thousands of casualties and immense numbers of refugees, like the Armenians shown here encamped in Syria.*

children on the street, it is possible that there were only few survivors of the city's Armenian population that would have attracted his attention or warranted his comment. Nevertheless, considering both the severity of the deportations as well as the paranoia with which Istanbul viewed the prospects of Armenian collaboration with the enemy, it remains somewhat puzzling and unclear why Mustafa failed to address the deportation and killings of Armenians in his journal during this time. In the context of his past experiences, as well as the limited number of writings he produced during this time, this absence of any mention of Armenians in his Diyarbakir diary is not entirely without precedent. Shortly after his arrival to the Gallipoli front, the CUP government enacted a similar policy of dispossession and deportation toward the region's native Greeks population. Within a few a weeks of the Allied assault on the peninsula, Mustafa Kemal would have most certainly witnessed, or at least had heard of, the mass removal of Orthodox Christians from villages and towns close to his headquarters. However, to date, no letter or document bearing his signature or name has emerged that gives any indication of his thoughts toward this policy.

It was only later, after World War I ended, that he offered some indication as to his opinions on the wartime deportations and massacres of Christians. Among his many speeches and interviews that were printed in the years after the collapse of the Ottoman Empire, Mustafa Kemal rarely referred directly to the CUP's deportation policies. In his famous 1927 speech, for example, he acknowledged the initiation of the deportations but insisted that his followers did not engage in massacres and had protected properties abandoned by Armenians ("some Armenians," he claimed somewhat cryptically, "had been saved from deportation").[9] Yet on this and other occasions, he declared that Armenians were not the victims of massacres either during the war or afterward. In both public and private, Mustafa Kemal declared that neither he nor the members of his postwar resistance movement, the National Forces, bore any ill intentions toward Armenians or Greeks residing in Anatolia. In his estimation, Russia, Great Britain, and France bore particular responsibility for both fanning the threat of Christian separatism and propagating false accusations toward the empire.

In one public address in December 1919, he offered this interpretation of Muslim–Christian relations during World War I:

> Whatever has befallen the non-Muslim elements living in our country is the result of the policies of separatism they pursued in a savage manner, when they allowed themselves to be made tools of foreign intrigues and abused their privileges. There are probably many reasons and excuses for the undesired events that have taken place in Turkey. And I want definitely to say that these events are on a level far removed from the many forms of oppression which are committed in the states of Europe without any excuse.[10]

Like other elements of Atatürk's past, it is difficult to isolate his actual or contemporary feelings or impressions of the CUP's wartime policies toward the empire's Christian population from the later context that informed the aforementioned comments. By the postwar era, foreign troops had occupied much of what remained of the Ottoman state and civil war had erupted in Anatolia. By the 1920s, no one within Mustafa Kemal's political circle would have disputed the notion that Muslims comprised both the heart and soul of the Ottoman nation. While Christians may have experienced hardships during the war, Muslim suffering, in his estimation, far outweighed the grievances of Armenians and Greeks. Acts of violence committed against Muslims in Anatolia during the Turkish War of Independence served to further impugn allegations of Ottoman transgressions against Christians in the preceding years. To suggest otherwise in Turkey by the 1920s was interpreted as rejecting the revolution that Atatürk had led and pardoning those who had inflicted defeat and partition upon the Ottoman Empire. In other words, to treat the deportation and massacre of Armenians as a crime against humanity was to detract from what he considered to be the inherent innocence of the early Turkish state.

A second topic barely touched upon in Mustafa Kemal's writings from 1916 is the status or political leanings of Kurds in the region. Kurds, who made up a large portion of the populations of provinces of Diyarbakir and surrounding provinces, are only mentioned in passing in his journal and letters from this period. In one letter to Corrine, he passed comment upon a Kurdish woman he encountered, who, in his words, had her hair cut in a "Kurdish way" and was dressed in a "very soiled dress" and possessed "equally [soiled] feet".[11] His reference to the impoverished state of the woman he chanced to meet south of Diyarbakir was emblematic of the impressions many Ottoman officers possessed of Kurds in general during this era. From the perspective of sophisticated officials raised or educated in the cities and towns of western Anatolia and the Balkans, the lands of southeastern Anatolia were among the most remote, backward, and impoverished corners of the empire. In keeping with this worldview, state functionaries and intellectuals correspondingly perceived the Kurds as reactionary, boorish, and recalcitrant in their temperament. The onset of World War I accentuated these elitist impressions. While some Kurds proved willing to answer Istanbul's call to arms, many others fled from military service or, worse still, collaborated with the invading Russians. As a result, the CUP government undertook a similar policy of deportation and relocation of Kurds in Diyarbakir and other areas of southeastern Anatolia. While seemingly not subject to the sort of depravations most commonly associated with the wartime policies targeting Armenians, large numbers of Kurds were transplanted from their homes to areas further west of the front. Yet, like the mass removal of Armenian, Greek Orthodox Christians, and other peoples in the region, CUP officials hoped that this deliberate re-engineering of Anatolia's population would mitigate the present and future threats of Kurdish rebellion and sedition. Mustafa Kemal's arrival to Diyarbakir in April 1916 corresponds to the period in which this policy began. However, for reasons that are not clear, he makes no reference at all to the CUP's Kurdish policies.

German influence over the conduct of the Ottoman war effort markedly increased during the course of Mustafa Kemal's tenure as an army commander in eastern Anatolia. Under the influence of Field Marshall Erich von Falkenhayn, whose failure outside of the French bastion of Verdun had earned him the epithet "the blood pump," Enver and his staff dispatched Ottoman troops to aid German offensive operations in Romania and Galicia. Despite the successes enjoyed by these forays into the German eastern front, the loss of these invaluable reinforcements detracted from Istanbul's ability to hold off British and Russian attacks in Iraq, eastern Anatolia, and on the Sinai Peninsula. In early 1917, von Falkenhayn and Enver colluded again in an ambitious plan to take the offensive against British colonial troops marching northward through Mesopotamia. The two agreed to form a new army group tasked with retaking Baghdad, which fell to the British in March 1917. The formation of this new army unit, dubbed the

Lightening Group (*Yıldırım Grubu*), included the Seventh Ottoman Army, led by the newly appointed *Pasha*, Mustafa Kemal.

The creation of the Lightening Group, and the prospect of a desperate assault on Baghdad, exacerbated mounting tensions between Mustafa Kemal, Enver, and the German officers stationed in Turkey. Since his departure from the Galipoli front, Mustafa had repeatedly called into question the empire's war aims and the roles played by Berlin's delegation of officers. In late 1915, he had circulated an encrypted memo to other high-ranking officers raising his objections to Istanbul's current military strategy and the overbearing interests of German officers. Official suspicions toward Mustafa Kemal were heightened following an attempted coup in early 1916. One of the plotters, Yakup Cemil, suggested under interrogation that the conspirators had hoped Kemal would assume Enver's role as minister of war once the coup was completed. His appointment to von Falkhenhayn's Lightening group further widened the gulf between Mustafa and his superior officers. In an extended report dispatched to Enver and the grand vizier's cabinet in September 1917, he railed against the military's handling of the conflict, which had inflicted poverty upon the empire's citizenry and brought about a wave of anarchy to the countryside. In terms of the conduct of the war itself, Mustafa Kemal offered this interpretation:

> Turkey's military situation is this: The army, compared to the initial stages of the war, is extraordinarily weak. Much of the army's existing forces are about a fifth of their required strength. The state's deficient man supply is not capable of reinforcement; so much so that, like the Seventh Army, it is not possible to maintain strength even in one army with all of the reinforcements and provisions found within the state.[12]

In addition to these reasons, as well as other challenges facing the Ottoman Empire on every front (including suspicions that Germany intended to colonize the Syrian provinces), he ultimately resigned from his post as an army commander and returned to Istanbul. There, he continued to stir discontent among generals and bureaucrats, complaining openly of the leadership of the CUP's governing triumvirate. Enver eventually confronted him and demanded that he either resign his commission in the army or no longer engage in politically contentious behavior.

Plans for an official visit to Germany by the Ottoman royal family provided some respite in Mustafa Kemal's strained relationship with his commanding officers. Assigned as an attendant to Prince Mehmet Vahdeddin's traveling entourage, he left Istanbul for Berlin in December 1917. Upon his arrival to Germany, Mustafa's reputation as a hero of the Gallipoli campaign had preceded him. Even Kaiser Wilhelm II took note of his presence upon his introduction to the host delegation. While basking in his notoriety, Kemal exercised little constraint before his German counterparts in voicing his disapproval of von Falkenhayn's plans for the *Yıldırım* Group. He personally pressed Vahdeddin to assume greater command of the military and reiterated his disapproval of the CUP's management of the war. Mustafa's private protestations bore no fruit and upon his return to Istanbul in early January 1918, he was once again ordered to return to duty on the Ottoman frontlines in Syria.

However, a severe infection in his left kidney prevented him from returning to active duty. Instead, Mustafa Kemal once again took leave to attend to his ailments. In May, he boarded a train bound for Vienna and took up residence in the town of Karlovy Vary (then known as Karslbad). While relaxing in the town's natural hot springs, Mustafa Kemal began to keep a diary. His "Karlsbad Memoirs," which were later published by his daughter Ayşe Afet İnan, offer a detailed account of his thoughts and opinions on the war, politics, and society, as well as his daily activities away from the front. In addition to carriage rides, reading books, and taking in the warm waters of the local baths, Mustafa engaged in deep discussions on a variety of issues facing the empire. In the company of his friend Cemal Pasha (who was also in Habsburg

Austria on holiday), he debated the meaning of "ideal of Turkishness (*Türklük mefkuresi*)," the opinions of the various peoples comprising the Arab lands and Central Asia (Türkistan), the conduct of Ottoman guerrilla units in Macedonia, as well as fiscal issues in Egypt.[13] He frequently references issues related to marriage, female companionship, and women's rights (although he confesses that did feel disposed toward marriage). It is also clear that his thoughts did not stray far from the challenges his adversaries within the Ottoman high command (particularly Enver) posed once he returned to Istanbul. Most strikingly, in a conversation with a female acquaintance, he reflected upon his desires and approaches toward reform within the Ottoman Empire:

> If I ever acquire great authority and power, I think that I would introduce at a single stroke the transformation needed in our social life. I do not accept and my spirit revolts at the idea entertained in some quarters that this can be done gradually by getting the common people and the *ulema* [Islamic clergy] to think at my level. After spending so many years acquiring higher education, enquiring into civilized social life and getting a taste for freedom, why should I descend to the level of common people? Rather I should raise them to my level. They should become like me, not I like them.[14]

In hindsight, Mustafa Kemal's early inclination toward "authority and power" appears strikingly prophetic. Atatürk, upon assuming the presidency of the Turkish Republic, did govern with the sort of confidence and conviction he displays within the pages of his Karlsbad diary. His writings from this period also affirm earlier displays of his intellectual curiosity and political awareness of events and trends both inside and outside of the empire. It also confirms his immediate aspirations to succeed Enver and the triumvirate in some capacity within the upper echelon of the Ottoman state (he had, while in Germany, for example, suggested to Vahdeddin that he could serve as minister of war under a new administration). Yet, given the hostilities he confronted from

more superior officers in the capital in 1918, there was no immediate indication that Mustafa Kemal would ever live to see himself assume the kind of authority he may have desired.

An inescapable air of crisis gripped the capital upon his return
from sick leave in August 1918. News that a last-ditch German offensive had failed along the Marne on the Western Front compounded Ottoman losses in Palestine and Iraq. Throughout the
spring, British troops, with the backing of an army of rebel Arab
cavalry units from western Arabia, pushed ever deeper into the
empire's Levantine provinces. The inability of Ottoman and
German officers to stave off the surrender of Jerusalem and Jericho
echoed the loss of further territory north of Baghdad. It is against
this backdrop that Mustafa Kemal rejoined the Lightening Army
Group, now led by his previous German commander, Liman von
Sanders. He enjoyed little glory or successes during his final
months as commander of the Seventh Ottoman Army. A British
offensive against Ottoman lines outside of Nablus in September
soundly shattered the left wing of the Lightning Group, forcing
von Saunders to withdraw further north without any hope of reinforcement or resupply. By the time advancing British units and
their Ottoman Arab allies entered Damascus on October 1, waves
of desertion had sapped von Sander's command of much of its
strength. In the waning days of October, the last of his troops,
numbering a little over 5,000, took up defensive positions just to
the south of Aleppo. Mustafa Kemal's bitterness over the army's
total disintegration prompted him to write a ferocious telegram to
Vahdeddin, who had assumed the Ottoman throne as Mehmet VI
in July 1918. He castigated Enver, Liman von Sanders, and other
superior officers for their ineptitude and cowardice. In the absence
of men willing or capable to fight, as well as officers competent
enough to lead them, there was "nothing left to do," in his estimation, "but to make peace."[15]

Despite thwarting hesitant British and Arab advances, Mustafa
Kemal's defense of Aleppo proved futile once news broke that
the war had come to an end. On October 30, 1918, Ottoman

representatives on the island of Mondros (or Lemnos) boarded the *HMS Agamemnon* in the hopes of seeking an armistice with the Entente. The terms of the Ottoman capitulation at Mondros were stark and uncompromising. In exchange for an end to armed hostilities, Istanbul agreed to withdraw all of its troops from positions beyond southern and eastern Anatolia or surrender to Allied forces. Entente forces demanded unhindered access to all Ottoman ports and railways, as well as fortified positions on the Bosphorus and Dardanelles Straits. In addition to the de facto loss of the empire's Arab lands, the Mondros agreement stipulated that the eastern six Armenian provinces of eastern Anatolia be formally under the protection of the war's victors. Lastly, in order to "defend the [empire's] borders and maintain public security," the Entente required all Ottoman army units to demobilize.[16]

The signing of the Mondros Armistice dealt a final and lasting blow to the CUP's triumvirate regime in Istanbul. Weeks in advance of Istanbul's surrender, Enver and Talat had vacated their positions as ministers of war and the interior. The two men, alongside one-time minister of the navy, Cemal Pasha, then fled the country aboard a German submarine two days after the ceasefire was finalized. Fears of being prosecuted for their roles in initiating the mass deportations of Armenians clearly weighed upon the minds of the CUP's leading figures in the weeks preceding their abandonment of the empire. In mid-October, Talat issued a degree allowing the return of exiled Armenians to their homes. This decision was finalized on November 4, three days after Enver, Talat, and Cemal fled the country, with the rescinding of the Deportation Laws of 1915. As the Allies (as they became more generally known after the war) took their first steps toward occupying what remained of the empire's Anatolian core in the winter of 1918–1919, scores of CUP officials and sympathizers would be arrested on charges of committing war crimes.

One can imagine that Mustafa Kemal did not mourn the collapse of the triumvirate's hold on power in Istanbul. If anything, the flight of Enver, Talat, and Cemal clearly confirmed his long-held position that the CUP regime's careless and arbitrary leadership had led the state to ruin. Speaking almost a year in advance of Istanbul's surrender, he declared to one journalist that "our own men in high office are gamblers, staking Turkey's destiny on the turn of the single card of final Germany victory. They are not aware that, at this moment, they have lost the war."[17] The fact that the CUP government did not survive Berlin's capitulation on November 11 is now often interpreted as a testament to his earlier clairvoyance.

Liman von Sander's departure from the Ottoman Empire paved the way for Mustafa to assume absolute command of the Lightning Army Group. His tenure as commander, however, lasted no more than a week. With the demobilization of his command on November 7, Kemal joined many other high-ranking Ottoman officers in returning to Istanbul. On the day of his arrival, November 13, 1918, the first Allied warships weighed

The Allies occupy the capital: British troops march through Istanbul after the war.

anchor off the shores of the capital. While the armistice made no reference nor offered any legal justification for the city's occupation, the Ottoman government, as well as what remained of the empire, henceforth would exist under a glass.

In his return to Istanbul, Mustafa Kemal joined an immense number of officers, enlisted men, and refugees who arrived in the capital after witnessing six intense years of combat and devastation. In the capital and in every corner of what was once the Ottoman state, the survivors of the conflict grappled with a series of bitter truths. World War I, coupled with the wars in the Balkans and in Libya, gave rise to all of the fears and threats that had lingered over the empire for more than a century. Decades of reform, particularly within the military, proved fruitless in staving off the collapse of the empire's forces. None of the victories achieved by the Ottoman army or navy over the course of the years between 1912 and 1918 could redeem the suffering and losses experienced by each and every inhabitant of the capital at war's end. The few successes achieved at Gallipoli, in eastern Anatolia, Iraq, Palestine, Galicia, Romania, Iran, and the Caucasus, did little to compensate for the territories lost or the hundreds of thousands of men killed, wounded, or left disease stricken. Even before the last battle was fought, the international press had publicized accounts of diplomatic discussions between Britain and France over the future of the Ottoman lands, leaving little doubt that the Allies intended to partition the empire among those who had supported or gleaned the sympathies of the war's victors. While the sultan and his offices remained nominally in control of his imperial domain, neither the sultanate, nor the state's military or bureaucracy, possessed any immediate leverage to negotiate the empire's future borders.

The abrupt departure of the CUP's governing triumvirate exacerbated the uncertainty and bitterness with which many individuals in Istanbul viewed their immediate political prospects. Mustafa Kemal's unswerving criticisms of the wartime government resonated strongly among various circles inside and outside of

the capital in the winter of 1919. Rather than serving as a tool
meant to unify the empire's diverse population and mobilize the
state's resources as a nation in arms, the war wrought virtually
unbridgeable political, economic, and social cleavages in every
corner of the country. Mobilization for war, in terms of both men
and material, devastated the imperial economy, causing widespread
outbreaks of famine, disease, and starvation. The mass displacement of Ottoman civilians and escalating patterns of desertion
from the army degraded the ability of the state to maintain law
and order, a phenomenon that left large swaths of the countryside
in the hands of bandits. Despite the suffering of countless citizens
living in both town and country, many within the CUP profited
from the war as contractors and purveyors of abandoned property (a phenomenon that Mustafa Kemal himself railed against in
his famed September 1917 report to the Ottoman government).
The deportation and death of thousands of non-Muslims, rather
than helping to secure the state, deprived local communities and
the national economy of workers and skilled professionals needed
in this time of profound crisis. As surviving Greek and Armenian
deportees returned home, state agents and local inhabitants were
forced to contend with conflicting claims over lost or stolen property as well as the guilt, tension, and uncertainty accompanying
the arrival of these accused traitors.

All in all, the empire that Mustafa Kemal and many others
had served over the course of these six years of fighting had
changed dramatically and irreversibly. The loss of his hometown
of Salonika, coupled with the displacement of his mother and
siblings, left little doubt that Istanbul was the only place that
Mustafa could rightfully call home. The Balkan Wars placed a
great many of his comrades in a similar predicament. The wartime
deportations of non-Muslims, a phenomenon rooted in longstanding official suspicions toward the loyalties of Christian groups
living throughout the empire, consummated a fundamental principle held by the Hamidian and CUP regimes: Muslims indeed
comprised the nucleus of the Ottoman nation. British General

Edmund Allenby's conquest of Palestine (a feat that was in part accomplished with the support of local rebels), as well as the loss of Iraq, compelled many of the remaining officers and officials in Istanbul to further refine their collective notions of the contours of the Muslim Ottoman nation. In the absence of large numbers of Arabic speakers, many with close ties to elite political circles in Istanbul, including Mustafa Kemal, perceived Anatolia, with its Turkish-speaking majority, as the last true and sustainable vestige of Ottoman patriotism and sovereignty.

In this ominous political climate, there was little immediate agreement within the capital on precisely who should wield power. Factionalism and confusion reigned within the ranks of the CUP in the wake of the triumvirate's decision to flee the country. While powerful figures like Enver and Talat hoped to influence the political affairs in the empire from exile, their political rivals remaining in the capital, including Mustafa Kemal, jockeyed for position in the hopes of assuming their place in office. Meanwhile, longtime opponents of the CUP, including those close to Sultan Mehmet VI Vahdeddin, worked to reverse the political tide brought on by the Revolution of 1908, staffing offices inside and outside the capital with anti-Unionist dissidents.

The fractiousness defining the struggle for power in the capital mirrored the even larger debate over how the empire should respond to the occupation of the city and the impending partition of the empire. Many members of Istanbul's political elite placed their faith in future diplomatic negotiations with the so-called Allies. With the support of Britain, France, or the United States, some hoped that a truncated, but viable, empire could somehow be retained. Some political dissidents in the capital, particularly those drawn from Armenian, Greek, Kurdish, and other populations, saw the prospect of an Allied-brokered settlement as a means of securing separate independent or autonomous states free from the capricious political policies that marked the CUP's reign over the empire. A significant number of officials and officers residing in Istanbul that winter disavowed any form of negotiation with the Allies. For this contingent, as well as their supporters in many of the empire's provinces, armed resistance was the only legitimate and honorable means of securing an acceptable resolution to the many crises facing the Ottoman nation.

Mustafa Kemal, in the six months immediately following the Mondros Armistice, did not resolutely support any single position on who should lead the empire. His stances on diplomatic negotiation with the Allies and the prospect of armed resistance also fluctuated during this critical period of time. His decision in May 1919 to abandon the capital and support the growing insurgent movement based in Anatolia left little doubt about his sympathies and future aspirations.

To understand how and why he resolved to leave Istanbul in 1919, a choice that ultimately placed him on the path to power as Turkey's first president, one must contend with ideas and experiences that shaped his service in the Ottoman army in World War I. The war, despite its attendant hardships, catapulted Mustafa Kemal upward through the ranks of the military. His bravery and fortitude outside of Gallipoli secured him a place as a triumphant hero at a time when few of the nation's generals enjoyed any success on the battlefield. Mustafa's consistency and competency as an army commander in eastern Anatolia and Palestine further sheltered him from the vitriol and disgrace that ruined the careers of high-ranking Ottoman officers who had failed at their posts on other fronts. Most important, his steadfast and overt opposition to the strategies and tactics advocated by Enver and his staff liberated Mustafa from any blame associated with the CUP's wartime policies. Unlike many of his superior commanders, the war, in the eyes of many of his contemporaries, defined Kemal as an independent and consummately loyal officer.

His often ill-tempered and quarrelsome relationships with German officers such as von Sanders and Falkenhayn were in part symptomatic of his antagonism toward prevailing CUP policies. In light of his experiences in Libya, the Balkans, and on various fronts during World War I, the antipathy he demonstrated toward

German advisors provides strong evidence of his general aversion to foreign interference in Ottoman affairs. Mustafa Kemal's contentious attitudes toward Ottoman independence (a tendency that resonated in his personal struggle for autonomy as a military commander) did not necessarily translate into an uncompromising bias against Western European cultures or political ideas. Despite repeated threats of resignation, Mustafa proved capable of compromise with his German counterparts at opportune times (as seen in his relationship with Liman von Sanders during the Gallipoli campaign). Moreover, his writings and activities in Sofia, Diyarbakir, and Karlsbad provide more than ample evidence of his affection and interest for ostensibly foreign sources of political and cultural inspiration. It should be said, however, that his sympathies for policies favoring women, as well as secular inclinations, were not entirely unique; many of his compatriots within the CUP, as well as a number of intellectuals and writers disassociated with state service, developed similar tastes and interests during this period of time.

Perhaps the most illuminating and fateful aspect of Mustafa Kemal's writings and behavior during the war is his attitude toward power and authority. Many of the anecdotes associated with his leadership as a frontline officer, as well as the political rancor he fostered among his superiors while away from the fighting, strongly affirm the confidence and conceit with which he perceived his native abilities to lead. The sense of entitlement that defined his perspectives upon military and political affairs, in hindsight, appears born out of both the successes he enjoyed while in command and the education he acquired from the books he read while at rest. It was only after the war was over, and more commonly after he became president, that many of his contemporaries began to interpret these elements of Kemal's personality as signs of his inborn ability to rule.

CHAPTER 3

|ATATÜRK AS A REVOLUTIONARY,|
1918–1922

In reality, in those days in which we found ourselves, the foundation of the Ottoman State had caved in. Its existence had come to an end. The Ottoman lands had been completely partitioned. In the middle, a homeland sheltering only a handful of Turks remained. It was not clear whether or not it was possible to save this area from partition. The Ottoman State, its independence, the sultan, the caliphate, government, all of these words lost their meaning. . . .

Gentlemen, in this situation, there was one only decision. That is, to establish a wholly independent, new Turkish state based upon international standards of sovereignty.[1]

MUSTAFA KEMAL UTTERED THESE WORDS in October 1927, almost four years after the establishment of the Republic of Turkey. This passage makes up only a small portion of a six-day-long speech he delivered before representatives of his governing Republican Peoples' Party. "The Speech," or *Nutuk* as it was later called, included a broad array of recollections and opinions regarding the struggle that led to the establishment of his government and the personal experiences that marked his ascendency to the post of president. Taken as a whole, the *Nutuk* renders an absolute and critical interpretation of the events, personalities, and tropes that defined the years between 1919 and 1927.

In reflecting back upon the first months following the close of World War I, Mustafa Kemal conveyed his unswerving belief that he alone best understood the challenges facing the peoples of the Ottoman Empire. Accordingly, he proposed that he alone possessed the will and grasped the means to right the ship of state. Beginning with his arrival to the port city of Samsun in May 1919, his speech provided a detailed account of his plans to lead a resistance movement bent upon creating the "wholly independent, new Turkish state" he eventually came to build and govern. A great number of daunting obstacles, he admitted, stood in his path as leader of this movement. Several foreign armies occupied Anatolia, each intending to stake an unjust claim to the empire's territorial core. His army, dubbed the National Forces (*Kuva-yı Milliye*), also contended with a host of domestic adversaries, including supporters of the corrupted sultan and Greek and Armenian separatists. There were also dissidents and reactionaries within his own camp who sought to undermine his leadership or thwart the National Forces' march toward victory. With the conclusion of what he called the "War of Independence" (*İstiklal Harbi*) in 1922, he proclaimed that his army, officers, and commanders had "completed one of the greatest feats in history."[2] Kemal, in drawing this chapter of his speech to a close, left little doubt that his determination and vision provided the momentum and foresight that inspired this final victory.

Despite the brevity of this portion of his life, no understanding of Atatürk's accomplishments and character is complete without a close and detailed analysis of his role as leader of the National Movement. The Turkish War of Independence (also known as the Greco-Turkish War of 1919–1922) was an exposition of his abilities as an astute politician, diplomat, and military commander. There is no denying the force of his personality in considering the many events and policies that proved instrumental in laying the foundation of the Turkish Republic. The war, both in terms of the fighting as well as the political wrangling that enveloped the conflict, equally molded and was impacted by Mustafa Kemal's political outlook and manner of governance. In reflecting on these years, it is clear that he viewed the war as a test that affirmed his rightful claim to power.

The recollections of his companions, as well as the research of contemporary scholars, do underscore and corroborate elements of Atatürk's interpretation of this formidable period. He, as leader of the National Movement, had achieved many feats deemed by many previously as improbable. He had undeniably helped to deliver Anatolia from Western occupation and annexation, an accomplishment seeminlgly unrivaled by any leader in the immediate postwar era. The nascent government he established in Ankara, which at first contested, but ultimately usurped, Istanbul's power and prerogatives, mirrored many of the constitutional and democratic traits found in Europe. By 1922, he was a leader who commanded genuine international recognition and respect, both for his leadership and his political vision.

Mustafa Kemal's contemporaries, and recently unearthed documentary evidence, do bare details that at times complicate and contradict the narrative found in the *Nutuk*. His path to assuming control of the National Forces, as well as the reasons behind his dramatic rise to political prominence, was not completely of his own doing. Once in command, Mustafa often betrayed an assertiveness and severity in dealing with political rivals and discontents. More important, many within society, particularly among common villagers and city dwellers, did not readily take to his style of leadership or support the political aspirations embodied by his National Forces. Both during the war as well as in the years succeeding it, Atatürk remained a controversial and divisive figure among those he claimed to represent and lead.

Days after returning from Syria, Mustafa Kemal settled into a house with his mother and sister in the Istanbul neighborhood of Şişli, a fairly new and affluent community located to the north of the capital's historic center. He spent much of the winter months of 1918 and 1919 visiting colleagues and senior officials in the hopes of securing a job within the post–Committee of Union and Progress (CUP) administration now governing Istanbul. Even before his arrival in the city, he had plied friends in the capital with requests to be considered for the post of minister of war, which had been vacated with Enver Pasha's departure. Later in November, he sought an audience with Mehmet Vahddedin, whom he hoped would include him in the formation of a new government. His desire to hold higher office in the capital had even compelled him to seek the intervention of representatives of the British occupation forces in the city, suggesting through an intermediary that he could assume the role of governor over the British-held mandate state in Anatolia. None of these overtures bore any fruit.

Seeking office drew only part of Kemal's attention during these uncertain days in the capital. It appears much of his time was spent in the company of friends, most of whom were fellow senior officers who had served along various fronts. The individuals with whom he visited and entertained in the months following the Mondros Armistice were equally occupied with new appointments or were pursuing other avenues of political influence. Together with his childhood friend Ali Fethi Okyar, Mustafa briefly assisted in the publication of a newspaper that focused upon issues related to the future of Ottoman sovereignty and government (a topic of increasing sensitivity following the sultan's decision to disband the parliament in December 1918). His public activism during this period of time reflects the intense and expansive nature of popular debate in the capital in the months after the empire's surrender to the Allies. The longing to maintain some semblance of political integrity within the empire compelled some current and former officials, as well intellectuals and social activists, to curry favor with Great Britain, forming such groups as the Association of the Friends of England. Some, including a few of Kemal's close colleagues, placed their faith in the creation of an American protectorate in Anatolia (a hope that was quashed with Washington's withdrawal from the League of Nations). Still others drawn from the empire's diverse ethnic and religious communities banded together to lobby the Allies to recognize the political and cultural rights of Kurds, Armenians, Greeks, Laz, Circassians, Albanians, and other groups. Still others shared in the sort of opinions espoused by Mustafa Kemal and his close friends in advocating their categorical opposition to any encroachment upon the state's integrity and independence. This latter group found a voice in the formation of a national congress (*Milli Kongre*) in Istanbul in November 1918, which was composed of a diverse array of prominent political figures.

The national congress assembled in Istanbul, in hindsight at least, represented a growing consensus within the ranks of the CUP's remaining supporters and sympathizers living in the empire's nominally surviving provinces. The desire to organize and carry out a campaign of armed resistance, based upon the formation of locally based national committees, had been among the contingency plans considered by leading members of the triumvirate government during the months leading up to the end of the war. With the assistance of the remnants of the Ottoman clandestine service, the notorious Special Organization, CUP agents stashed large caches of arms and munitions in various locations throughout Anatolia in anticipation of an invasion and occupation by the Allies. In such far-flung cities as Kars, Edirne, and Adana, groups of officers, politicians, activists, and religious leaders aligned with this network of resistors, which was named the Karakol Association in 1918, continued to pool their resources for this likely struggle after the flight of the principal members of the CUP regime.

As conditions in the Ottoman Anatolian countryside worsened between January and May 1919, Karakol efforts toward mobilizing an armed response assumed greater urgency. French troops in the southern districts of Mersin, Adana, and Maraş gained control over the southern Anatolian region of Cilicia. Thousands of displaced Armenians joined the French administration, stoking tensions among Muslim townspeople and villagers. Small garrisons of British, Italian, and French soldiers taking up positions in Edirne, Antalya, Çanakkale, and Batum also sent forays and intelligence agents into the Anatolian interior to gather information on banditry and the treatment of returning Christian deportees. These piecemeal encroachments upon the sovereignty and integrity of Ottoman Anatolia foreshadowed the looming threat posed by rumors of an imminent Greek invasion from across the Aegean. Athens, which had joined the Allies during the final stages of the war, had long curried territorial designs upon portions of Ottoman Anatolia and Thrace. Before the Paris Peace Conference in January 1919, Greek Prime Minister Eleftherios Venizelos maintained that the war validated Greece's right to occupy all Ottoman lands inhabited by Greek-speaking Christians (a proposition rooted in the so-called *Megali Idea*, Greece's long-standing irredentist policy of expansion into the Ottoman lands). With the consent of Great Britain, Venizelos authorized the landing of thousands of Greek troops on the Ottoman port of Izmir on May 15, 1919. Within two weeks of the landing, Greek expeditionary forces advanced deep into the coastal province of Aydın, leaving hundreds of Muslim civilians dead and thousands more displaced.

A great number of officers and bureaucrats with close ties to CUP resistance efforts in the provinces surrounded Mustafa Kemal during the weeks preceding the Greek invasion. Prominent commanders such as Ali Fuat Cebesoy (who commanded troops in central Anatolia) and Kazim Karabekir (commander of Ottoman forces in the eastern city of Erzurum) purportedly sought his support and participation in their efforts in leading armed resistance groups in the interior. He had even entertained, and reportedly denied, overtures from one of the principal organizers of the Karakol Association, Kara Kemal. On April 30, 1919, he accepted an appointment as an inspector of the Ninth Army group based in the eastern Anatolian town of Erzurum. Before departing, Mehmet Vahdeddin received him one last time at his court. The sultan wished Mustafa well in assuming his new post, which nominally entailed overseeing the demobilization of Ottoman troops and maintaining law and order in the far-off province.

Mustafa Kemal disembarked from the steamship *Bandırma* onto the shores of the Black Sea town Samsun on May 19, 1919. In reciting his *Nutuk*, he recalled his first steps on the beaches of Samsun as the moment in which he commenced his participation in the resistance to liberate Anatolia from occupation. However, his narration of the events immediately leading to his departure from Istanbul that May is rather vague. He portrays his decision to assume the post of inspector of the Ottoman Ninth Army as the obvious result of his comprehension of the crises facing the nation; it was, he contended, his duty to abandon the capital and join those brave men who were preparing to cast out the armies that had invaded and occupied the land. Moreover, he offers no explanation for how or why his appointment to Erzurum afforded him the opportunity to eventually lead his National Forces against the Greek, British, and French forces that opposed him. In retrospect, the context of Mustafa Kemal's arrival to Samsun is of critical importance to his emergence as president and founder of the Republic of Turkey. Considering the significance with which he alludes to his landing at Samsun (to the point that he later claimed, somewhat erroneously, that May 19 was in fact his birthday), at what point did his assignment to Erzurum become his mandate to lead both the National Forces and, thereafter, the Turkish nation?

Contemporary observers and modern scholars point to several factors that precipitated his departure to Anatolia. Mustafa Kemal, as a result of his heroism at Gallipoli and on the Syrian front, was a general held in high esteem within the ranks of the Ottoman army. Perhaps of greatest importance, he was also an individual with profoundly independent political leanings. While his relationship with the CUP spanned much of his professional career, his reputation for obstinacy, and his vocal criticisms of the wartime triumvirate government, allowed Mustafa to present himself as a conciliatory figure in the eyes of CUP opponents. It is for this reason that the sultan, who loathed and feared the Young Turks, sought his counsel and entrusted him with his assignment to Erzurum. Kemal's ability to straddle Istanbul's fractured political landscape, it appears, allowed him to both glean the trust of militant CUP activists (individuals who ultimately comprised the core of the National Forces) as well as gain the confidence of the sultan and others who opposed the committee's return to power (thus allowing him to escape to Anatolia without garnering any untoward suspicions).

While Atatürk's ability to mollify the sultan's fears and attract the attention of CUP supporters may help explain his candidacy to lead the National Forces, it does not sufficiently clarify how he, as opposed to other officers, was entrusted with command over the resistance movement taking shape in Anatolia at this critical juncture in time. Mustafa Kemal was not the only officer in the empire with an impressive professional pedigree or a reputation as a skilled battlefield commander. His friend Ali Fuat Cebesoy, as well as other CUP luminaries such as Rauf Orbay (former minister of the navy), possessed equally impressive credentials. Both of these individuals also had participated in the organization of the Karakol's militant activities months in advance of Kemal's departure for Samsun. Moreover, from the perspective of those within the CUP in early 1919, it was unclear whether Enver, who remained popular with the ranks of the military, would return to the empire to lead the fight against the Allied invasion.

Circumstantial evidence suggests that his informal promotion to command the nascent units of the National Forces in the spring of 1919 was perhaps the result of ad hoc planning and negotiation. Mustafa Kemal was in constant communication with individuals with close ties with the Ministry of War, which was an early focal point of resistance efforts in the Ottoman provinces of Anatolia. Many of the officers staffing the ministry, as well as those still without an official appointment, maintained direct and indirect connections with exiled members of the CUP, including Enver and Talat Pashas. Once he arrived in Samsun and gathered a handful of like-minded officers around him, several prominent figures associated with the initial organization of the resistance movement (such as Talat and the leaders of the Karakol) readily accepted Mustafa's assumption of authority.

While the precise moment Mustafa Kemal received the right to command remains unclear, it seems reasonable to suggest the CUP, as both a party and as a movement, was critical to his ability to accede to the role of leader of the nascent National Forces. Though the CUP had formally ceased to exist in early November 1918, British intelligence officials maintained that the party continued to survive intact and direct clandestine activities in the capital and throughout various provinces. British agents, in surveying the capability and strength of the CUP in January 1919, made no reference to Mustafa Kemal, suggesting instead that a cabal of figures (as opposed to one de facto head) managed the party's internal affairs. One British intelligence agent posed that, despite the fragmentation of authority within the upper ranks of the Young Turks, the CUP's highly centralized "linked-grouped system" of internal organization allowed party activists to coordinate their efforts with some degree of cohesion.[3] Whenever Mustafa did finally assume the mantle of leadership for the National Forces (be it before or after his arrival to Samsun), the available evidence suggests that the CUP's supple internal structure, once at his disposal, allowed him to command with an immense amount of breadth and authority.

Kemal's first weeks in Anatolia passed with little fanfare or action. Much of his time was devoted to touring the towns and villages in the immediate hinterlands of Samsun, a region that had been racked by paramilitary violence and banditry. Greece's expanding occupation in the Aegean provinces outside of Izmir appears to have prompted him to take direct and definitive action. In late May, he dispatched a secret telegram to local officials

throughout Anatolia outlining his evaluation of the current political situation and recommending a unified course of action:

> The occupation of Izmir and Manisa by the Greeks and of Antalya
> and Konya by the Italians is making the situation continuously
> worse. Samsun and Trabzon will soon meet the same fate. Armenia
> now has the dream of a large empire. The central government is
> like a prisoner under Entente occupation. It is necessary to join
> with Turkish administrators to take over the defense of our inde-
> pendence. If foreigners occupy the East, it is necessary to use gen-
> darmes and soldiers to resist them. I believe the nation is capable of
> rescuing itself from imprisonment, of living independent in its
> lands in defending its rights and independence. . . . It is necessary
> to make preparations now; to increase the number of men in your
> forces; and bring together all available arms.[4]

Similar commands and recommendations emanated from Mustafa's
camp outside of Samsun over the next two weeks. In mid-June,
two of his close comrades from Istanbul, Ali Fuat Cebesoy and
Rauf Orbay, joined him in the inland town of Amasya. From this
relatively quiet and secure location, the men issued a joint statement now referred to as the Amasya Circular. The document,
which was partially released to the press, further expounded
upon the immediate dangers facing the Ottoman state from the
threat of foreign occupation. In the absence of a government
free from outside intervention, Mustafa Kemal called for the convening of a congress to be held in the eastern Anatolian town of
Sivas. Once at Sivas, delegates from throughout the remaining
territories of the empire would assume the task of raising and
organizing the national resistance forces beginning to take shape
in various corners of Anatolia.

The Amasya Circular heightened the fears of British commanders and the sultan's retainers alike. British field officers who
had encountered Mustafa Kemal during his tour of the Black Sea
region issued multiple reports expressing their suspicions that

he and other high-ranking army offices were intent upon initiating an armed insurgency. Occupational authorities in Istanbul agreed with these assessments and attempted to compel Ottoman ministers to remove Mustafa Kemal from command. Similar apprehensions were found among elements of regular imperial administration in the capital. The prospect of open rebellion in inner Anatolia, the sultan and others feared, would only detract from the ability of the empire to negotiate an amicable peace with the Allies at Paris.

Mustafa Kemal preempted calls for his dismissal and arrest with his formal resignation from the Ottoman army in July 1919. Now dawning civilian clothing, he journeyed in the company of his close companions to the town of Erzurum. The decision to travel to Erzurum coincided with the assembly of a separate congress of officers, clerics, and notables organized by one of Mustafa's senior associates, Kazim Karabekir. As an early participant in Karakol's resistance efforts, Karabekir, purportedly with some reluctance, obliged two members invited to the conference to relinquish their seats so that Kemal and Rauf Orbay could formally participate in the proceedings. Others protested the attendance of the former army inspector on the grounds that he was a military officer and that his attendance was decided without the consent of the body as a whole. With Karabekir's vocal support, Mustafa Kemal allayed these fears and assumed the post of president of the meeting. The Erzurum Congress, which met from July 23 to August 7, debated and passed a number of core resolutions pertaining to the defense of eastern Anatolia from invasion and partition. The body, which comprised fifty-four representatives from throughout eastern Anatolia's so-called six provinces, echoed the calls of the Amasya circular, declaring that the government was held captive by an occupying force seeking to conquer and divide the empire. It expressly reputed the terms of the Mondros Armistice that assured special consideration for Armenians in eastern Anatolia. Neither Armenians nor Greeks living in the empire would receive special treatment or territorial concessions in resolving the current crisis. While the Erzurum Congress sought to guarantee the "lives, property, and honor" of non-Muslims still living in the empire, participants in the assembly contended that the supposed existence of a Muslim majority in eastern Anatolia necessitated the region's retention as Ottoman territory.[5] In concluding the meeting, representatives established a formal organization called the Defense of Rights Society and agreed to the creation of a "representative committee" tasked with uniting all resistors under the umbrella society's leadership. "All Muslim countrymen," the congress instructed, were "natural members" of the Defense of Rights.[6]

Sultan Mehmet VI, as well many of his supporters in the Sublime Porte, viewed the Erzurum Congress as final confirmation of Mustafa Kemal's intransigence. By royal decree, he was stripped of his rank and military honors and declared a rebel in defiance of the sultan. Mustafa Kemal and his collaborators in the representative committee of the Defense of Rights Society greeted Istanbul's condemnation in silence. Their work on the behalf of the Ottoman nation remained transfixed upon the liberation of the sultan and his state. Despite Istanbul's continued opposition to their activities, Mustafa Kemal and his supporters did not deviate from their formal position on the maintenance of an independent and viable Ottoman Empire with the sultan/caliph as its rightful sovereign.

A second national congress assembled in September in Sivas, an event that had been anticipated with passage of the Amasya Circular. Like the meeting in Erzurum, Mustafa Kemal again presided as president of the gathering (a position that was again contested as undemocratic by some members of the group). The rhetoric and resolutions of the Sivas convention mirrored those discussed two months earlier. On this occasion, the Defense of Rights Society called upon a unified defense of all of Anatolia as well as Eastern Thrace, the empire's last toehold in southeastern Europe. It formally denoted that "all Islamic elements" living in the Ottoman lands were "true brothers, imbued with feelings of mutual respect and sacrifice for each other, and wholly respectful of racial and social rights and local conditions."[7] Both the Istanbul government and the forces occupying Anatolia and Thrace were obliged to accept the existence and indivisibility of this Muslim majority that favored the independence and sovereignty of what remained of the Ottoman Empire. While delegates at Sivas did debate the possibility of an American mandate in Anatolia (since Washington had no clear or direct interest in Ottoman affairs), Mustafa Kemal and the Representative Committee of the Defense of Rights Society concurred that the National Forces should accept only political or material aid from the United States or another state in the hopes of maintaining the autonomy of the movement.

For an event that claimed a national mandate, the Sivas meeting attracted fewer participants than the proceedings in Erzurum (fighting and political uncertainty prevented most of the invited guests from attending). The presence of only thirty-eight delegates did not inhibit Mustafa from tightening his grip upon the emerging leadership of the National Forces. In the midst of the congress, he pointedly confronted one of the founders and leaders of the Karakol resistance network, Kara Vasif. Kemal publicly admonished Vasif for his participation in the organization, charging that he and other Karakol agents had employed his name without receiving his authority as head of the Defense of Rights Society. Vasif responded disconcertedly to these claims and assured Mustafa Kemal that he, and he alone, was in command of the National Forces. Recent scholarship suggests that this exchange between the two men, which resulted in the abrogation of the Karakol Association, represented one of Atatürk's overtures toward consolidating his political position. Kemal most certainly knew of the organization's earlier activities in organizing resistance groups in Anatolia and was aware that it gleaned the support of both rank-and-file CUP officials as well as members of the wartime triumvirate government. According to Vasif, both Enver and Talat supported Mustafa's leadership within the emerging National

An Assembly of Patriots. *Members of the Sivas Congress, including Mustafa Kemal (seated in the middle of the bottom row), pose for a portrait commemorating the event.*

Forces despite his recent accession to the resistance. The meeting at Sivas, it seems, allowed him an important opportunity to distance himself from the former leaders of the CUP and assert a definitive claim of authority over the individuals and networks comprising the Defense of Rights Society.

The quorum Mustafa Kemal attained at Sivas in September 1919 placed his Defense of Rights Society firmly at the head of several ragtag armies already in action in the far western province of Anatolia. In the province of Aydın, a stable front, comprised of regular Ottoman army units and irregular militias, had formed a cordon around the Greek beachhead based in Izmir. By the fall of that year, a cohort of local bureaucrats, Muslim clerics, landowners, and merchants had assembled similar congresses in the small towns of Balıkesir and Alaşehir, bodies that assumed immediate control over the logistical and administrative needs of the Aydın theater of operations. Fears of a Greek invasion across the Thracian frontier compelled a clique of army officers, public officials, and local notables in Edirne to mobilize troops in defense of the province. Clandestine efforts to arm militias and local military units had also commenced in French-occupied territories of southern Anatolia. Kemal's assumption of authority, coupled with Karakol's closure, placed the efforts of military and civilian resistance leaders in Edirne and Aydın at the disposal of the Defense of Rights Society's Representative Committee, leading to a new, increasingly more unified command structure. While Karakol's elimination may have led to a transition in authority at the heights of the National Forces at this stage in the conflict, personal relationships and political ties first forged before and during the war by the CUP continued to undergird the bonds within armies and assemblies composing these resistance efforts. The principal members of the Mustafa Kemal's representative committee, such as Rauf Orbay, Bekir Sami Kundukh, and Refet Bele, were each prominent figures with the CUP at the war's end. Several key members of the representative committee were personal acquaintances, close friends, or former comrades-in-arms with leading officers and officials in western Anatolia. The ability of Mustafa Kemal and his supporters to sustain a united front against Greek and other foreign forces at this juncture, despite the limited amount of time separating the end of the war and the establishment of the Defense of Rights Society, remained deeply indebted to the organizational and interpersonal attributes of the CUP.

The growing integration of combat units under the command of Mustafa Kemal in the fall of 1919 compelled a shift in policy in Istanbul among the sultan's supporters. Rather than directly seeking to stamp out the Defense of Rights Society or seek open confrontation with the National Forces, a new grand vizier called for the opening of a new Ottoman parliament. With the election of new parliamentary representatives, the sultan and his supporters hoped to recall prominent supporters of the National Forces to the capital and place the movement more closely to imperial centers of power. After several months of fierce campaigning, voters in the Anatolia provinces returned over a hundred representatives to the assembly, the vast majority comprising supporters of the Defense of Rights (including members of the Representative Committee). Voters in Erzurum elected Mustafa Kemal representative of their district but, out of fear of arrest, he opted not to take his seat in the assembly. Nevertheless, once representatives convened the first sessions of parliament in January 1920, the body's political agenda echoed many of the tenets established in Erzurum and Sivas. In a declaration passed by the body on February 17, parliament reiterated the Defense of Rights Society's rejection of the postwar foreign occupation of Ottoman lands. It advocated that local populations under Allied administration, including the Arabic-speaking territories south of Anatolia, be allowed to vote, as a plebiscite, on the political future of their lands. The creation of plebiscites was demanded in other territories occupied before World War I (such as western Thrace and districts in the south Caucasus). The assembly pledged to uphold the rights of "minorities" (mostly meaning Christian groups) in the empire "on condition that Muslim minorities in neighbouring countries" received the same protections.[8]

Present-day commentators and scholars have commonly referred to the Ottoman parliament's February declaration, referred to at the time as the National Pact (*Misak-i Milli*), as a document that provided the territorial and rhetorical basis for the Republic of Turkey's establishment in 1923. Future negotiations between Mustafa Kemal and the Allies, as many have correctly suggested, were premised upon the assertions of popular sovereignty and independence with the various lands mentioned within the February 17 pronouncement. The National Pact expressly references postwar treaties with the state of "Turkey," as opposed to the Ottoman Empire, a feature that provides a subtle hint of the emergence of the republic yet to come. When viewed in its immediate context, the National Pact agreed upon by the Ottoman parliament stands as a testament to immediate desires of many in Istanbul to retain all or as much of the imperial lands that had existed in the antebellum period. While French and British troops may have seized the empire's predominantly Arab provinces (a conquest formally avowed with the signing of the Treaty of San Remo in April 1920), neither the Istanbul government nor proponents of the National Forces were completely willing to concede the loss. The presumption that the empire could obtain bordering regions in the Balkans and the Caucasus through plebiscites did not completely represent a departure from past Ottoman policies; during World War I, CUP policymakers had hoped to reintegrate territories lost in the late nineteenth and early twentieth centuries back into the imperial whole. Most important, the National Pact made clear that no change in government, regardless of the state of the nation, was forthcoming. The parliament, in outlining the territorial basis for the maintenance of Ottoman sovereignty, unequivocally calls for the protection of the "Ottoman sultanate" and the "Islamic caliphate" in Istanbul from "every danger."[9]

What is more puzzling and difficult to explain is the National Pact's use of the term "Turkey" in reference to the empire the document claims to defend. Many names had been associated with the empire since its conception in 1299. While formal internal or diplomatic documents tended to use the "Ottoman" moniker to describe the state over which the sultan claimed governance, Western Europeans also tended to employ the terms "Turkey" and "Turks" in referencing the place and people where the Ottoman Turkish language was spoken. By the nineteenth century, government officials and private citizens inside and outside of Istanbul began to use "Turkey" and "Turks" interchangeably with the Ottoman state and Ottomans in general. Mustafa Kemal's own choice of words reflects an ambivalence toward the exclusive ethnic connotations of the terms "Turks" and "Turkey." Through his writings and declarations before, during, and immediately after the war, there appears to be no discernable difference in his usage of the terms "Turkey" and "the Ottoman Empire"; the two states are one and the same. His appeals or references to Turks also possess ambiguous connotations. A Turk, depending on the context, denotes a Turkish-speaking Muslim, a Muslim of any ethnic extraction, or, in some cases, any Ottoman citizen regardless of one's language or religion.

The ambiguity and contradiction that beset the meaning of the terms "Turkey," "Turkish," and "Turk," in some ways, relates to official formulation of Ottoman nationalism under the reign of Abdülhamid II and the Young Turks. While many officers, bureaucrats, and intellectuals, including Mustafa Kemal, continued to acknowledge the inherent linguistic and religious diversity of the empire, World War I appeared to further solidify the position of Muslims (particularly Turkish speakers) within the core of the Ottoman state and nation. Debate over the future of postwar Europe helped to simplify, to some degree, internal debates on identity and political autonomy in the Ottoman lands. In embracing Woodrow Wilson's insistence upon self-determination for national groups throughout the former imperial domains in the Habsburg lands, negotiators in Paris readily adapted their demands to the tune of supposed demographic majorities existing within various locales. For supporters of the National Forces, including Mustafa Kemal, the current consensus in Versailles allowed for the supposition that the Ottoman parliament, and by extension the Defense of Rights Society, indeed represented the will of Muslims and Turks. In an interview with an American journalist in 1920, Kemal took particular issue with the application of the Wilsonian doctrine of self-determination:

> Have President Wilson's Fourteen Points survived? If so, why were they not applied to making the peace with Turkey? Why was the principle of self-determination applied to the Armenians and the Greeks in Turkey and not to the Turks? Where is the fair play of civilized Europe, which condemns the Turk? The peace terms were conceived by imperialists without regard to the principles of justice.[10]

According to the Nationalist reading of the Wilsonian principles of self-determination, minorities, such as Greeks and Armenians, had to accept the existence of a "Turkish" (mostly meaning Muslim here) majority within the political borders enveloping the territories claimed by the National Pact. In short, while the National Pact may have not provided a blueprint for the empire's demise and the erection of a republic in its place, the Ottoman parliament did lay the foundation of a national discourse that privileged Muslims, and, to a large degree, Turkish speakers, as the sole arbiters of the region's future.

The reformation of an Ottoman parliament with overt sympathies for Mustafa Kemal's National Forces greatly unsettled Allied representatives based in Istanbul. Rather than pacifying militant opposition to the occupation and restoring the sultan's ascendency within the Ottoman government, the parliamentary election of late 1919 appeared to lend greater legitimacy and independence to Mustafa Kemal's activism in Anatolia. Anger within Mehmet VI's court resulted in the March appointment of a new grand vizier, Damat Ferid, who, as head of the Sublime Porte in 1919, had demonstrated a strong antipathy for the CUP and the National Forces. British authorities, with tangential support of the Greek and French governments, also moved in March to officially suppress expressions of support for the Nationalists in Istanbul. On March 16, 1920, British General George Milne formally declared the Ottoman capital under Allied occupation. British forces, which had been garrisoned in the city for over a year, utilized the decree as license to round up and arrest prominent and outspoken members of the parliament and civil society with ties to the Defense of Rights Society. Over a hundred and fifty suspects, including Mustafa's close associates Rauf Orbay, Fethi Okyar, and Ali Çetinkaya, were then remanded to a prison on the island of Malta. The imposition of a formal occupation of the capital, as well as Damat Ferid's appointment to head the Ottoman civil government, incited an exodus of activists and officials from the city. Two days after the commencement of Allied rule over Istanbul, Ottoman parliamentarians held their last session with most deciding, en masse, to flee the capital.

Mustafa Kemal did not stay idle in the midst of parliament's last meetings and the onset of British control of Istanbul. In December, he, as well other firm supporters of the Sivas Congress, had shifted their base of operations to the central Anatolian town of Ankara. His isolation from machinations of the Ottoman parliament did not deter him from his efforts at marshaling men and material for militias at the front or lobbying local officials for political support. Nevertheless, Kemal's decision to exclude himself from the opening of parliament exposed his uncomfortable and relatively insecure relationship with the Ottoman government. As a private citizen, his standing within the Defense of Rights Society and its Representative Committee did not invest him with any official powers. He, alongside other retired officials and intellectuals, was no more than a prominent activist with ties to men of direct political influence. His activism, beginning with the convening of the Erzurum conference, had been in defiance of the government despite the fact that he insisted that he and others were acting in the defense of the Ottoman state. Without assuming his seat in the assembly, the legality of his actions, let alone his status within the National Forces, was tenuous in principle.

General Milne's appropriation of power over the capital, as well as the Ottoman government's complicity in the closure of parliament, offered Mustafa Kemal a welcome and needed pretext in assuming greater control over the direction and solvency of the Anatolian resistance movement. Within a day of the legislature's last session, he circulated a telegram to officials throughout the empire calling for new elections and the resumption of the assembly's activities in Ankara, his new base of operations. For parliamentarians escaping from Istanbul, Kemal's offer of sanctuary could not come at a more opportune time.

There were some members, such as the assembly's president, who opposed the transference of the legislature's activities to the Anatolian hinterland. Despite these objections, Mustafa presided as the first president over the reinstated Grand National Assembly in late April 1920. It was an event possessing an ironic air of imperial decorum (complete with prayers and salutations in the name of the Prophet Mohammed and the Sultan Mehmet VI) despite being declared a body of rebels and infidels by officials in Istanbul. Mustafa Kemal, as president, posed that neither he nor other members of the Ankara legislature were in defiance of the sultan. The Grand National Assembly instead represented the will of the Ottoman nation at a time when foreign forces (themselves true infidels) held the sultan and his government in Istanbul in captivity. The chief Islamist jurist in Ankara, as well as over 200 other scholars throughout Anatolia, issued their own ruling (or fatwa) contesting the claim of Mustafa Kemal's aposty from Islam.

Over the next several months, the Grand National Assembly set out to establish a parallel system of government, usurping virtually all of Istanbul's administrative prerogatives. Laws were immediately passed in April creating departments of health, economy, justice, education, and security. New parochial and professional schools were opened and new taxes, agricultural protocols, and civil services (such as refugee relief and care for orphaned children) were initiated under the auspices of Ankara's authority. The Grand National Assembly also oversaw the imposition of new stringent laws outlining acts of treason, laws often used to prosecute opponents of the National Forces. Nevertheless, lawmakers in the assembly left little doubt as to what state they represented. Upon the letterhead of official correspondence, the empire's official name, the Sublime Ottoman State (*Devlet-i Aliye-i Osmaniye*), remained in currency. For much of the early existence of the body, assembly members upheld the rules of conduct and order set out by the Ottoman constitution of 1876. The legal basis of the Grand National Assembly arrived at an important crossroads in January 1921 with passage of a provisional constitution (known as the Law of Fundamental Organization or *Teşkilat-ı Esasiye Kanunu*) formally outlining the mandates of the Ankara legislature. While expressly stipulating that the Grand National Assembly represented the "continuation of the Ottoman Parliament," the constitution did not make mention of the sultan's administrative status or relationship with respect to the laws and motions passed. The first article stated, much to the dismay of supporters of the sultan, that "rule belongs to the nation" and that the "form of administration would be based upon the wishes of the people."[11]

After 1923, Mustafa Kemal suggested that the formation of the Ankara government and the establishment of a new constitution provided the first concrete step toward the foundation of a republic in what remained of the Ottoman lands. Other statements attributed to him and other Nationalists from the early state of the Turkish War of Independence suggest that he had hoped to transfer imperial authority from Istanbul to Ankara in the event of a national resistance. Nothing in Mustafa Kemal's official statements or acts in 1920, or during any other year during the War of Independence, suggests that the formation of the Turkish Republic was a part of some grand strategy. When viewed from the context of the experiences and events of World War I, the opening of the Ankara government, as well as the consummation of a constitutional order exclusive of the influence of the sultan's offices, was not altogether unprecedented. CUP planners had contemplated moving the capital of the empire to the Anatolian interior (either to Ankara or to Konya) toward the latter stages of World War I. The Counter-Revolution of 1909, which resulted in Abdülhamid II's removal from power, had established a pattern of governance in the empire that reduced the sultan to little more than a ceremonial position divested of real power. In some respects, the administration Mustafa Kemal oversaw in the War of Independence represented less of a revolution and more of a continuation along the trajectory established by the CUP. Moreover, few acts passed by the wartime Grand National Assembly entailed the sort of political or social revolutionary changes later realized during the first decades of the Turkish Republic. Religious law (or şeriat) remained entrenched within the civil and criminal codes of the early Ankara regime. While elements of the contemporary Ottoman press had debated issues of women's rights, language reform, and the ethno-national character of Anatolia,

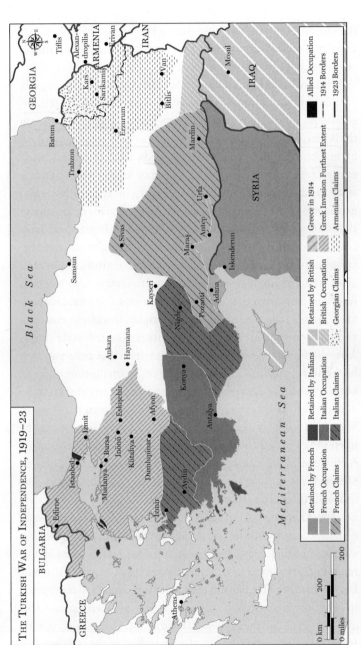

MAP 2. The Turkish War of Independence, 1919–1923

91

the Grand National Assembly, during these years of war and occupation, made no effort to transform the political or cultural
attributes of Ottoman society.

Ankara's growing influence over the Anatolian countryside
particularly complicated matters of diplomacy. In May 1920, negotiations in the Italian town of San Remo concluded between
the Allies, resulting in a framework for the near total annexation
of the Ottoman Empire into foreign hands. Later in August, a delegation from Istanbul journeyed to France to sign a formal peace
treaty with the Allies. Dubbed the Treaty of Sèvres, the agreement formally ratified the creation of British and French mandate
states in the former Ottoman lands of Syria, Palestine, and Iraq.
Greek, British, French, and Italian zones of occupation were recognized, provisions that included direct recognition of Greece's
claims to Ottoman territory in eastern Thrace and western
Anatolia. The Treaty of Sèvres also validated the establishment
of an Armenian state with territorial rights in eastern Anatolia
and held open the possibility of a future Kurdish state in the
Anatolian provinces adjacent to British Iraq. The sultan was allowed to remain in Istanbul and govern a smattering of lands
within the core of Anatolia (although the sultan's right to rule
depended upon his compliance with the terms of the treaty).
These and other concessions offered by Mehmet VI's government
in Istanbul helped to reinforce Ankara's nationalist credentials.
By the end of 1920, few outside of Istanbul could rightfully view
Mehmet VI and his supporters as anything less than collaborators with the Allied occupation.

The Ankara administration complemented its opposition to
Allied discussions at San Remo, and the resulting Treaty of Sèvres,
with its own diplomatic initiatives. In the face of the Allies' determination to assume territorial concessions from the Ottoman
Empire, Mustafa Kemal and his supporters possessed few poten-

tial supporters in the international community with power and
influence. Within the Nationalist camp, there was a strong consensus of opinion that the sole state with the means and desire to

aid the Nationalist cause in Anatolia was Russia. Changes in policy from Moscow following the establishment of the Bolshevik government in 1917, from the perspective of Mustafa Kemal and others, gave credence to such a conclusion. Lenin, who categorically rejected imperial Russia's expansionist policies of the prewar era, foreswore claims to Ottoman territory. The anti-imperial tenor of the Bolshevik cause had resulted in the outbreak of war between Moscow and the Allies, with French, British, American, and Japanese troops seizing peripheral portions of the Russian state. Shared interests and common enemies had led CUP officials to seek Bolshevik support in the early stages of the Nationalist struggle, providing the earliest channels of communication between Moscow and Mustafa Kemal's circle of resistors. In May 1920, the Ankara government dispatched its first embassy to Moscow in the hopes of receiving aid and political recognition from Lenin's government.

Over the course of the following year, negotiations between the two sides ebbed and flowed. Bolshevik representatives assured the Ankara delegates of their support for a politically and economically independent Turkish state. Yet Bolshevik support, by the late summer of 1920, came with the proviso that Ankara cede portions of the lands of eastern Anatolia to an independent Armenian state. Mustafa Kemal rejected the demand out of hand. Perhaps more worrying for Kemal (who abhorred Communism) as well as other members of the Grand National Assembly, was the prospective influence Russian agents and domestic Communists would glean with the signing of an alliance between the two governments. Many in the ranks of the Defense of Rights Society outwardly advocated Communist and Socialist ideas, a trend that Bolshevik officials did indeed hope to exploit in their favor. By the summer of 1920, a Communist faction calling itself the National Front had established itself in the Grand National Assembly. With pro-Bolshevik forces gathering strength inside and outside of the Ankara government, Mustafa risked losing control over the Nationalist cause in the name of receiving needed external support and recognition from the Soviet Union.

Nationalist successes on the battlefield helped to finalize an agreement between the Bolsheviks and the Ankara government. In September 1920, Kazim Karabekir, under the direction of Mustafa Kemal, marched his army based in Erzurum east against the forces of the nascent Democratic Republic of Armenia. After crossing the borders allotted to the Armenian state in the Treaty of Sèvres, his men marched on the cities of Kars, Ardahan, and Artvin, three regions previously seized by the Russian Empire in 1878. Armenian forces, with little outside military support, signed a ceasefire with Karabekir two months after the opening of hostilities. A Bolshevik invasion of Armenia in November helped to finalize the exchange of territory completed by the Nationalist offensive in September. In March 1921, the Bolsheviks and Kemal's Nationalists consummated their relationship with the signing of the Treaty of Moscow. The agreement negated all previous agreements between the Ottoman Empire and imperial Russia and established a mutually recognized border between Turkey (a term used specifically in the treaty) and the future Soviet Republics of Georgia, Armenia, and Azerbaijan. At the price of receiving arms and international recognition from a state equally engaged in a struggle against international imperialism, negotiators on the behalf of the Grand National Assembly were compelled to compromise on elements of the National Pact. The lands surrounding the city of Batum (a region seized by the Russian Empire in 1878) was ceded to the Republic of Georgia.

In the midst of Ankara's negotiation with Moscow over the future borders of eastern Anatolia, stiff resistance from the National Forces provided a similar pretext for a rapprochement between the Grand National Assembly and French occupational authorities. French control over the districts of Maraş, Urfa, Antep, and Adana began to weaken in the winter of 1920 despite the support lent by locally recruited Armenian militias. In January, detachments of the National Forces, in cooperation with local Muslim residents, raised a rebellion in Maraş and besieged French troops inside the city. The two sides agreed to a truce in February, leading to France's withdrawal from the town and the flight of thousands of Armenians in tow. Violence intensified in the region after the Maraş withdrawal as Armenian irregulars attacked Muslim villages and towns in Adana and elsewhere. Nationalist troops, under Mustafa Kemal's personal direction in the field, resumed the offensive against the French between April and October, seizing several French strongholds in the Taurus Mountains. Paris, in recognition of its weakened position in southern Anatolia, opened direct diplomatic talks with Ankara in the spring of 1920. Negotiations between Ankara and the French, like in the case of the Bolsheviks, progressed piecemeal over the course of a twelve-month period. While eager to withdraw from much of the areas claimed in the National Pact, French emissaries continued to seek assurances from Ankara regarding French territorial rights in Syria as well as economic interests in what remained of Ottoman Anatolia. Mustafa Kemal, who at times dealt directly with French representatives, adamantly contended that the National Pact, which entailed full territorial and economic sovereignty over Anatolia, remained the basis for any full cessation of hostilities. After an abortive attempt at a resolution in March 1921, French and Nationalist negotiators relented and signed a final accord in October 1921. Per the Treaty of Ankara, France agreed to withdraw all of its troops south of a line below the city of Urfa into the lands of Mandate Syria. Like the Treaty of Moscow, Ankara offered its own concessions, allowing for French control to remain over the districts of Antakya and Iskenderun (two cities claimed in the National Pact) and the extension of specific French economic rights within the borders of Anatolia.

Ankara's combined successes on the diplomatic and military fronts through 1920 and 1921, which also included the peaceful withdrawal of Italian occupational troops, elevated Mustafa Kemal's status as a statesman and military commander outside of the Ottoman Empire. In Germany, one newspaper joyfully greeted the successes "the Anatolians won under Kemal" in beating upon the "dirty, greedy outstretched claws" of the Great

Powers.[12] Editors at the *New York Times*, while condemning "the Turk" as a "convicted criminal incapable of reform," also offered a begrudging respect for the leader of the Nationalist cause. "Mustapha Kemal," in the paper's estimation, seemed to possess the "spirit that built the great Turkish Empire," and "as a national patriot one may admire him, even while realizing that his cause is about the worst in the world."[13] Support for Mustafa Kemal and the National Forces was strongest and most categorical among Muslim activists beyond the borders of the Ottoman Empire. Ahmad al-Sharif al Sanusi, one of the leaders of the anti-Italian resistance in Libya, visited Anatolia during the War of Independence and actively spoke on behalf of the Ankara government. Muslim activists in British India, who viewed the preservation of the Ottoman caliph as a critical symbol for the unification of Muslims against imperial rule throughout the world, also lent monetary and moral support to the National Movement. Mustafa Kemal reciprocated this support through his frequent appeals for greater unity among the Muslims of the world.

British observers voiced similar begrudging tokens of admiration in the midst of the occupation. As early as February 1920, within weeks of the official takeover of the capital, British intelligence officers offered a highly pessimistic interpretation of the Allies' position in Anatolia. British forces, as well as other Allied troops, were stretched thin with little hope for reinforcement. Financial constraints, as well as war-weary public opinion back at home, further eroded the ability of the Allies to maintain a long-standing presence in Anatolia. Mustafa Kemal, by contrast, "could await the moment when the economic and general political situation amongst the Allies" would preclude "further interference in his country." With prosecution of a dogged guerrilla campaign in the western, southern, and eastern portions of the empire, time was on Mustafa Kemal's side.[14]

Popular opinion within the Ottoman Empire did not uniformly match the admiration and respect Mustafa Kemal often elicited from foreign commentators. By far the most undeterred critics of the National Movement, and Mustafa Kemal in particular, were native Christians living inside and outside the National Forces' zones of control. Despite pledges to the contrary, Greek and Armenian Christian leaders and notables frequently expressed their fears in print and among foreign observers that a Nationalist victory would result in massacres and deportations of all non-Muslims. To the shock and chagrin of many within the Nationalist camp, such opinions gained currency among Muslims in various portions of Anatolia as well. The gathering strength of the National Forces in late 1919 and early 1920 prompted various degrees of opposition and suspicion in villages and towns devastated by the impact of World War I. Nationalist troops often demanded heavy taxes and further terms of conscription from Muslim families and communities that had shouldered immense financial and personal burdens during the previous war. Many local communities accused Nationalist officers of gross acts of corruption and exploitation, charges that often stemmed from previous terms of service as local officials under the wartime CUP government. Worse still, suspicion reigned in various corners of Anatolia regarding Mustafa Kemal's ultimate motivations in leading the National Movement. Many communities suspected that a Nationalist victory would lead to the return of the CUP, the party that had pushed the empire to the point of collapse in the first place. Still others feared that Kemal sought to usurp the Ottoman throne for himself, a charge frequently exploited by supporters of the Sultan Mehmet VI.

Popular opposition toward the Nationalist Forces resulted in successive rebellions throughout Anatolia between 1919 and 1921. In western Anatolia, rebels under the leadership of Ahmet Anzavur, a former gendarmerie officer and Istanbul loyalist, harried Nationalist detachments between fall of 1919 and the summer of 1920. As a force comprising both Muslim and Christian insurgents, Anzavur's forces garnered considerable support from local communities at odds with the prospective return of the CUP. Similar sentiments in the summer of 1920 spurred the outbreak of violence in Yozgat, a central Anatolian town synonymous with the anti-CUP activities of the prominent Çapanoğlu family. Further acts of rebellion were staged in 1921 along the eastern Black Sea coast and the mountainous region of Dersim, located immediately west of the Nationalist stronghold of Erzurum. In both of these later uprisings, fear of a CUP/Nationalist takeover (which would result, many suspected, in massacres and deportations) compelled both Muslims and Christians to drive Ankara's representatives out of the region. The Istanbul government, in the hopes of fanning the flames of popular opposition, fielded its own army against the National Forces based to the east of the capital. However, this so-called Disciplinary Force, which marched against Izmit in the spring of 1920, received little direct popular support.

Each of these rebellions was met with stern and often brutal acts of suppression by Nationalist troops. Despite the fact that the uprisings were spawned by the fallout of World War I and, to a large degree, represented the deep-seated apprehensions of both local Christians as well as certain Muslim minorities (such as Kurds, Circassians, and others), the Ankara government depicted each of these acts of rural opposition as the result of foreign meddling. Rebel leaders, such as Ahmet Anzavur, as well as their followers, were deemed reactionaries under the influence of duplicitous Ottoman officials such as Damat Ferid and financed by the British occupational authorities.

While the National Forces proved capable of defeating the uprisings staged between 1919 and 1921, the early successes of many disorganized and poorly armed rebel groups underscored critical weaknesses within the ranks of the National Forces. Much like the British and French occupational forces in the west and south of the country, Ankara's troops were thinly dispersed across Anatolia. Shortages in arms, money, and other resources further compounded Ankara's lack of available, as well as dependable, soldiers. The shortcomings of the National Forces proved detrimental in June 1920, when Greek expeditionary units broke out of their beachhead outside of Izmir and pushed steadily eastward across the Anatolian hinterland. Greece's decision to expand their zone of occupation, a stroke reluctantly agreed upon by London, put Ankara immediately on the defensive. By early July, Greek troops entered the cities of Bursa and Balıkesir, two vital Nationalist command-and-control centers. National Forces in eastern Thrace met similar reversals during a simultaneous Greek thrust that June. By the end of the summer, the Istanbul government formally ceded all territories now under Greek occupation, which included much of western Anatolia and most of Thrace up to the outskirts of capital, as part of the final negotiation of the Treaty of Sèvres.

Mustafa Kemal and the Grand National Assembly refused to relinquish any claim to the lands seized by Greece in the summer offensive of 1920 and set out to evict the Greeks by all means possible. Ankara commissioned the organization of several "flying

TAKING CHARGE OF THE BATTLE. *Mustafa Kemal dons his uniform one last time ahead of his army's final engagement with Greek troops.*

columns" tasked with undermining the Greek army's internal lines of communication and control within the environs of Balıkesir, Soma, and other western towns. A bitter guerrilla war ensued throughout the Greek occupation zone, as Nationalist insurgents, Greek regular troops, and locally armed militias traded strikes and raids. Muslim and Christian civilians bore the brunt of much of the fighting, with Greek troops and local collaborators beating, extorting, deporting, and killing large numbers of individuals suspected of sympathizing with the Nationalist cause. Muslim villagers also fell prey to Nationalist guerrillas and independent bandit gangs operating under the auspices of the Greek occupation. A controlled Greek withdrawal along their northern lines outside of Izmit and Bursa in summer of 1921 resulted in the worst of the atrocities committed against local civilians during the course of the occupation. According to both Ottoman and international studies conducted in the immediate aftermath of the Greek retreat, Greek troops and local auxiliaries (many of them composed of local Muslim and Christian recruits) murdered hundreds of Muslim civilians. In ceding the lands back to the Nationalist units to the east, Greek soldiers left scores of villages destroyed and forced thousands to flee for their lives.

The loss of Thrace and much of western Anatolia at the hands of the Greeks occurred at a time when Mustafa Kemal's own leadership within the National Movement appeared increasingly uncertain. Tension within the assembly mounted over the course of 1920 as Mustafa appeared increasing unwilling to cede power to rival politicians. Among those who initially spoiled for greater autonomy and influence in Ankara were Socialists and Communist sympathizers, a group that enjoyed greater political significance with the opening of direct relations with the Bolsheviks. The weight of this faction in the capital was further amplified with the support of the National Forces' most powerful and successful unit, the so-called Mobile Forces of Çerkes Ethem (or Ethem the Circassian). Ethem's role in crushing many of the revolts against the National Movement in western and central Anatolia in 1920 heightened his status as a political and military force that rivaled the units under Mustafa Kemal's more direct control. Fearing a direct challenge to his authority, Mustafa responded to this rising faction within the ranks of the National Movement with both words and deeds. In helping to craft a provisional constitution for the Grand National Assembly, Kemal and his supporters adopted multiple planks that resonated with the growing leftist consensus in Ankara. Many of his speeches and official statements from this period echoed leftist references to the threats of Western imperialism and capitalism. He complemented these steps by allowing for the creation of a separate Socialist coalition within the assembly (dubbed the People's Front) and the establishment of an independent Communist Party. The inclusion of several of the president's loyalists into the ranks of these coalitions unsettled many leftists allied with the People's Front and the Communists, opening rifts that benefited Mustafa Kemal's unitary influence over politics in Ankara.

The increasing fragmentation of leftist factions in the assembly, which earlier had relied upon the support of the Mobile Forces in the field, did little to undermine the independence and authority of Çerkes Ethem. Ethem's ability to wield influence in Ankara, as well as conduct operations as an exclusive detachment of the National Forces, was put on display in an assault on Greek lines in October 1920. After briefly seizing the western Anatolian town of Gediz, Ethem's forces staged an uncoordinated withdrawal alongside the bulk of the Nationalist army, resulting in heavy casualties and further territorial losses. When Mustafa Kemal suggested to one of his subordinates that Ethem, as well as his brother Reşit, a member of the Grand National Assembly, could be transferred to the Nationalist embassy in Moscow, the two brothers accused Mustafa Kemal of attempting to establish a dictatorship. As tensions between Ethem and Ankara mounted, Mustafa Kemal issued orders demanding the integration of his Mobile Forces into the regular Nationalist army command structure. When he refused, the commander of the Nationalist western front, İsmet, struck out against Ethem's base of operations in the town of Kütahya. Rather than put up a fight, Ethem, as well as his brothers, decided in February 1921 to head west across the frontlines and surrender his command to the Greeks. While Çerkes Ethem's defection occurred at a moment of profound uncertainty in Ankara's war against Greece, the conclusion of the controversy surrounding the status of the Mobile Forces ultimately strengthened Mustafa Kemal's hand over the direction of the National Movement. No substantial military force remained outside of Ankara's authority after Ethem's surrender, a trend that had begun with the closure of the Karakol resistance network. Mustafa Kemal's forces, which mostly comprised the remnants of the regular Ottoman army, thus had finally displaced the influence of the older militia groups previously formed by CUP activists, leading to an absolute monopoly over military affairs in the Nationalist camp.

Communist and Socialist opposition within the Grand National Assembly represented, in some respects, the possibility of a far more ominous challenge to Mustafa Kemal's leadership over the National Movement. Since his departure from Istanbul in the winter of 1918, Enver Pasha had not completely abandoned hope of returning to the empire. Between 1918 and 1920, he shuttled back and forth between Berlin and Moscow in the hopes of inspiring (and perhaps leading) anti-occupation efforts in Anatolia. He remained in steady contact with activists, politicians, and militants with ties to the CUP living in the Ottoman lands and in exile throughout this period. Enver and his supporters, while establishing a close association with the Bolshevik Party in Russia, aligned themselves closely with Communist and Islamist sympathizers in Central Europe and the Russian Caucasus. His attempts to forge this grand alliance equally served his aspirations to galvanize Muslim resistors throughout the world to unite against the dual threats of Western imperialism and anti-Bolshevik forces (which would equally aid him in his efforts to return to Ottoman Anatolia). From Ankara's vantage point, Enver's activism abroad held direct implications over the direction and organization of the National Movement. Enver, despite his failings as a member of the wartime triumvirate government, remained a popular and charismatic figure among rank-and-file fighters and administrators within the National Forces (particularly those with leftist leanings). As evidenced from statements made after the conclusion of the Turkish War of Independence, Mustafa Kemal's antipathy toward the former minister of war did not dull with the end of World War I. Moreover, it is clear he placed little faith in the Islamist/Communist consensus building abroad as a potential ally in the fight against foreign occupation in Anatolia. In a letter to Cemal Pasha, with whom Kemal had remained in contact up until his assassination by an Armenian activist in 1921, he explicitly warned his friend and former patron to "examine the reality of a revolt based on Islam."[15]

Fortunately for Mustafa Kemal, two events helped to preempt Enver's return to Anatolia. The signing of the pact of mutual recognition and assistance between Moscow and Ankara in March 1921 signaled an end of direct Bolshevik support for the former minister of war's desire to lead resistance efforts in Anatolia. Later that year, Enver journeyed to Batum in the hopes of crossing the border back into the empire. Yet, with the prospect of a Nationalist victory against the Greeks appearing ever more promising, the Nationalist governor of the neighboring province of Trabzon vowed to interdict his entry from the Caucasus. The former CUP leader, in the face of local Nationalist opposition, demurred from returning home and abandoned Batum after two weeks of waiting on the other side of the frontier. Unable to return home, and with no patron to support him, Enver traveled to Central Asia in the hopes of leading a rebellion among Muslim anti-Bolshevik dissidents. His final demise, which resulted from bullet wounds inflicted during a skirmish with Russian troops, came over a year later in a village found within the contemporary borders of Tajikistan. Mustafa Kemal's greatest rival ultimately returned home in 1996, when his remains were reinterred in an Istanbul cemetery attached to the Monument of Liberty, a memorial established in 1909 in commemoration of those who had died suppressing Abdülhamid II's counterrevolutionary putsch.

Mustafa Kemal's ability to maintain his supreme position within the National Movement ultimately rested with his ability to secure a final victory over the Greek invasion force residing to the west of Ankara. Between January and March 1921, Nationalist and Greek forces repeatedly clashed outside the village of İnönü to the immediate west of the town of Eskişehir. Despite fierce Greek resistance, İsmet's men mustered a series of counterattacks that resulted in the seizure of a crucial hill overlooking the village. The battle marked the first definitive victory over the Greeks, an event marked with celebrations in Ankara and the promotion of İsmet to the rank of *Pasha*. Over a decade later, he appropriated İnönü as his surname in commemoration of the place where he first attained fame as a warrior in the defense of the National Movement.

The Greek army under General Anastasios Papoulas remained undaunted in the aftermath of the fighting outside of İnönü. His men continued to press on into the spring and summer of 1921, eventually seizing the towns of Afyon, Kütahya, and Eskişehir. The loss of these vital urban centers quickly reversed the mood in the Nationalist capital as fears of a Greek offensive against Ankara itself appeared more imminent. In this hour of uncertainty, debate raged within the Grand National Assembly as officers and politicians began to appeal to Mustafa Kemal to take direct control over the front. As president of the assembly, Mustafa, for most of the conflict, interceded into military affairs only occasionally and often indirectly, choosing instead to busy himself with internal political matters within the chamber itself. The threat of an imminent Greek attack on Ankara, coupled with increasing rates of desertion among the foot soldiers manning the front lines, compelled him to act quickly and decisively. In August, after considerable debate, the Grand National Assembly approved a proposal making Mustafa Kemal commander in chief of all Nationalist troops, a position that gave him sweeping powers beyond leading troops into battle. Entrenched Nationalist units outside of Ankara continued to suffer setbacks in the weeks after Kemal established his headquarters close to the front. More heavily armed and better equipped Greek forces kept up their assault into August, at one point seizing the Nationalist fortifications at Çal Dağı, a key ridge above the Sakarya River. The capture of Çal Dağı shook Mustafa Kemal and Nationalist high command. According to subsequent accounts, Kemal and his subordinates contemplated withdrawing further toward Ankara after the loss of this critical piece of ground. As fate would have it, similar doubts reigned within Papoulas's camp. Within a matter of days of the capture of Çal Dağı, Greek troops began to retreat toward Eskişehir, paving the way for a Nationalist counterattack that reclaimed the high ground above the Sakarya.

The Battle of Sakarya, as the clash was later called, marked an important military and political victory for both the National Movement and Mustafa Kemal in particular. The Greek advance into Anatolia reached its high watermark along the Sakarya River in September 1921. While the war continued to rage between Greek and National troops on multiple fronts for another twelve months, no further attacks would threaten the security of the Grand National Assembly in Ankara. For Kemal, the battle of Sakarya solidified his political position both within the Nationalist government as well as within the army he now commanded. Soon after the battle, the Grand National Assembly awarded Mustafa Kemal with a promotion to the rank of field marshal, a title that placed him definitively at the heights of the National Forces (despite the fact that he had forfeited his commission in the Ottoman military years earlier). The assembly also bestowed upon him the title of "gazi," an honor of deep historical significance for field commanders in the Ottoman Empire. In assuming this mantle of a gazi, a title usually reserved for warriors of the Islamic faith, the Grand National Assembly included Mustafa Kemal Pasha within the same company of the first sultans of the Ottoman Empire as well as a select number of the heroes of the Ottoman military from the nineteenth century. There were, indeed, many within the Nationalist camp that had begun to doubt Kemal's leadership before the battle of Sakarya. While this opinion did not completely dissipate after September 1921, his victory that summer against the Greeks, coupled with the sweeping powers he had gleaned from the assembly before the battle, granted Mustafa Kemal an almost unquestioned position of leadership as the Turkish War of Independence was drawing to a close.

The political and military balance of power between Greece and the Nationalist government shifted steadily in Ankara in the twelve months following Sakarya. As the two armies remained dug in along a line to the east of Eskişehir, morale and material began to waver and decline among Anastasios Papoulas's forces. Diplomatically, Athens appeared increasingly isolated as Greece's erstwhile Allies, France and Great Britain, undertook greater consideration in seeking a diplomatic solution over the war in Anatolia. British authorities in Istanbul, who previously had offered direct and tacit support for the Greek invasion, recognized by the winter of 1922 that the front outside of Ankara was untenable and advocated a complete Greek withdrawal in order to forestall the near-certain military and human catastrophe that would follow. Doubts also pervaded the heights of the Greek government. Andrew, the crown prince of Greece, lamented privately that his government had to act quickly in order to remove Greece "from the nightmare of Asia Minor."[16]

Meanwhile, Mustafa Kemal, having escaped the threat of a complete military collapse, utilized the pause and staged a general mobilization of men and supplies in the territories controlled by the Grand National Assembly. In doing so, he retained his post as commander in chief, a step that roiled many of his rivals in the assembly. The Gazi's critics in the assembly, who in the months preceding Sakarya had formed a de facto political party called the Second Group, received further encouragement with the arrival of Rauf Orbay to Ankara. After his release from a British prison on the island of Malta, Rauf openly expressed many of the complaints levied by Kemal's opponents and pointedly asked if "it was possible if a person could be both head of the Grand National Assembly and commander-in-chief."[17] Mustafa, despite further complaints that he spent too much time in Ankara and not enough at the front, dismissed his challengers' complaints and continued to function as the Nationalist Movement's chief administrator and field general.

As he and his trusted lieutenants prepared for a grand offensive against the Greek lines outside of Eskişehir in the summer of 1922, Nationalist units moved against several remaining quarters of military resistance in central and eastern Anatolia. In addition to suppressing an uprising by the Kurdish and Armenian inhabitants of Dersim, Nationalist guerrilla units staged attacks against centers of native Greek Orthodox resistance along the coast of the Black Sea (an offensive that resulted in the deportations and massacres of Orthodox Christian civilians in the towns of Samsun, Merzifon, and elsewhere). Greek occupational forces in western Anatolia and Thrace staged similar acts of retribution and violence against Muslim villagers and townspeople in Bursa and Edirne as the war entered its third year.

The Turkish War of Independence achieved its grand climax on August 26, 1922. In the weeks preceding Mustafa Kemal's orders to attack, Nationalist units had feigned several maneuvers suggesting a coming assault to the north of the actual point of attack. When men of the First and Second Army Corps finally commenced their offensive outside the town of Kütahya, the Greek high command, as well as troops entrenched at the front, were caught completely by surprise. The Greek troops near the village of Dumlupınar, after withstanding an intense bombardment of their lines, broke ranks within a day of the battle's first volleys. General Georgios Hatzianestis, who assumed Papoulas's command in the spring of 1922, attempted to withdraw his men in good order westward toward the Aegean Sea. With the initiative now in hand, Nationalist cavalry and infantry units continued to press forward without relent. Unable to counterattack, and with few supplies left in their possession, the Greek retreat degenerated into full flight by the first days of September. The Greek route led to an absolute breakdown of law and order in western Anatolia as the battle lines surged toward the port of Izmir. Whole villages and towns were razed as Greek soldiers set fires and executed civilians in their wake. Nationalist troops seized large numbers of prisoners and in some cases exacted acts of revenge against captives and civilians alike. The Asia Minor Catastrophe, as it later became known in Greece, culminated in a bloody finale after Nationalist troops entered Izmir on September 9. Despite the fact that Greek soldiers had largely vacated the city, and Nationalist authorities had forbade acts of retribution, riots broke out among Nationalist soldiers, irregulars, and civilians, leading to numerous cases of looting and murder (including the lynching of an Orthodox archbishop). Four days into the Nationalist occupation, a fire erupted in the city's Armenian quarter. The blaze, which may have been intentionally set by Nationalists or local Muslims, continued to burn for days, ultimately claiming three-quarters of the city's buildings. Mustafa Kemal, who had arrived in Izmir a day after Nationalist troops entered the city, left town in the midst of the fire. He purportedly expressed little emotion in seeing the port go up in flames, cryptically stating, "Let it burn, let it crash down."[18]

One may interpret the Gazi's words in two ways. The destruction of this port on the Aegean, which had acquired the epithet "gavur Izmir," or infidel Izmir, was an event that marked the annihilation of Orthodox Christian life in the city. The fire, which leveled the old Greek and Armenian sections of the town, displaced much of Izmir's Christian population. The fire clearly resonated strongly with Mustafa Kemal in the aftermath of the battles and atrocities preceding and succeeding the Nationalist offensive of August 1922. The Turkish War of Independence was a dramatic exposition of intercommunal conflict in Anatolia. The war, which resulted in the mass expulsion, murder, and abuse of Muslim and non-Muslim civilians across Asia Minor, concluded a decade-long struggle over the fate of the Ottoman lands.

Throughout this ten-year period, opposing armies, militias, and mobs had committed innumerable atrocities across the Balkans, the Arab lands, the Caucasus, and Anatolia. While Kemal explicitly reprimanded the commander of the Nationalist forces in Izmir for his role in fomenting attacks against members of the native Orthodox population, his comments do suggest that the leader of the Nationalist government did bear some enmity toward his adversaries at the close of the war. The Greek army, as well as many of their local auxiliaries and supporters, did deny quarter to Muslim civilians as they advanced and retreated across Anatolia. Now that Izmir, which had been the central bastion of the Greek occupation, lay in ruins, one may suppose that the Gazi, at least in part, felt little sympathy for the Christians that bore the brunt of the disaster.

Mustafa Kemal's apparent indifference to the Izmir fire may have also represented an even more profound sense of resolution following the eviction of Greek forces. The Turkish War of Independence fundamentally demolished or undermined the political, economic, and social order that once had prevailed over the Ottoman Empire. Even at the time of his return from Syria in the days after the Mondros Armistice, an empire governed from Istanbul still existed. The empire at the end of 1918 still held a nominal claim to the lands of Syria, Iraq, and Hijaz to the south and continued to wield power over Anatolia and eastern Thrace. Anatolian society at the end of World War I still comprised an intricate patchwork of Muslim and Christian communities that had coexisted peacefully over the course of many centuries. Even though World War I and the Armenian deportations had greatly unsettled this diverse landscape, the Ottoman parliament in 1918 still possessed Muslim, Orthodox, and Armenian members tasked with representing a variety of diverse constituencies. World War I may have devastated large portions of Anatolia, as well as the Levant and Mesopotamia, but large portions of western Anatolia, which was among the most culturally and economically vibrant territories in the empire, were left unscarred by 1918.

"Let it Burn, Let it Crash Down." *The ruins of Izmir after Mustafa Kemal's army entered the town in the fall of 1922.*

The four years that followed the imposition of an Allied armistice at Mondros permanently shattered the imperial order. Despite some initial ties between the National Movement and resistance groups in Syria and Iraq, the political divisions rendered by the Treaty of Sèvres irrevocably severed Anatolia's bonds to the Arab lands. An insurmountable political divide surfaced within Asia Minor as well; a conflict that pitted the sultan and his supporters in Istanbul against the remnants of the CUP. As old Unionists reinvented themselves into members of the National Movement, a state of civil war wracked a variety of towns and villages. Many provincial communities, groups that included both Muslims and Christians, refused to accept the National Movement as anything other than an attempt by the CUP to resurrect itself despite its disastrous leadership during World War I. The British, Greek, Armenian, and French occupations proved even more polarizing. Between 1919 and 1922, Muslim and Christian communities in the environs Kars, Urfa, Bursa, and elsewhere were torn asunder. The struggle between occupational and National forces, from all sides, came to be interpreted largely as a sectarian conflict with little room for compromise. In settling the overarching questions confronting the political and territorial future of what remained of the Ottoman Empire, no corner of Anatolia was left unscathed by violence. Mustafa Kemal, in reflecting upon Izmir's destruction, suggested that the war, and its attending consequences, had run its full course. So much had been lost and damaged as a result of the conflict that it was impossible, and perhaps undesirable, for the old order to be restored.

While Kemal had indicated both publicly and privately that the state reached an important crossroads during the course of the conflict with Greece and the Allied powers, neither he, nor any of his supporters, appeared to have committed themselves to abolishing or dramatically altering any of the political pillars undergirding the empire. The Ottoman state, despite the profound territorial losses it had incurred as a result of World War I, remained nominally intact even in the waning days of the War of Independence. Even though the sultan and his immediate retainers had sought to undermine or reverse the political influence of the National Movement, the political leaders who had formed around Mustafa Kemal staunchly maintained that the war was fought in the name of the state they had served in advance of the Mondros Armistice. Nevertheless, the War of Independence did validate two political trends that signaled a forthcoming transformation in the nature of governance in Anatolia. Both of these trends first manifested themselves in the years before the war and were the direct result of the revolution brought about by the CUP in 1908. While Mustafa Kemal eventually laid exclusive claim to these emerging political tendencies, a closer inspection of the history of the late Ottoman Empire suggests that he was a direct beneficiary of the course of events, rather than the sole author of the revolutionary developments to come.

First and foremost, the war permanently and irreversibly deposed the sultan and his offices of genuine political power. The Young Turk Revolution of 1908 comprised the first steps that led to the emasculation of the sultan's imperial prerogatives. With the overthrow of Abdülhamid II one year later, the authority of the sultan was further degraded. The establishment of a CUP dictatorship in 1913 gave still greater authority to the Unionist-controlled parliament, rendering the sultan little more than a figurehead standing above the empire. As a consequence of the end of World War I, Mehmet VI enjoyed an unparalleled opportunity to reassert the royal family's status and influence. The remnants of the CUP, a collective that included Mustafa Kemal, did not accept this reversal of their political fortunes. In undertaking a concerted campaign against foreign occupation, Kemal and other Nationalist activists sought to contest the sultan's resurgent base of authority. The internal debate that raged between Mehmet VI and the Nationalist leadership over how to confront the Allied occupation thinly masked a profound rift concerning the nature of political control over the future of the empire. In colluding with the Allies, the sultan and his allies staked their political hopes on the collapse of the National Movement. The National Movement, in turn, transferred the empire's legislative branch to Ankara in an effort to both maintain the independence of this old bastion of the CUP and affirm their credentials as the true defenders of the imperial state. Greece's defeat in 1922 ultimately decided this contest of political wills, leaving Mustafa Kemal and the Grand National Assembly in firm control over most of Anatolia.

The second trend that assumed greater significance over the course of the War of Independence was the concerted use of Turkey as the name of the state encompassing what remained of the Ottoman lands. As previously mentioned, people both inside and outside of the empire used the terms "Turkey" and "the Ottoman State" interchangeably decades in advance of 1918. With the outbreak of the War of Independence, Nationalists slowly began to dispense with the latter title in favor of the former. This change occurred, it appears, without debate or formal approval. In the absence of evidence to the contrary, one may argue that the increasing use of "Turkey" within popular and official parlance within

Nationalist circles was emblematic of ideological and social leanings that had emerged first during the reign of Abdülhamid II and the Young Turks. The empire, in the minds of many critical CUP figures, was a state buttressed by the loyalty of its Muslim, Turkish-speaking majority. The Wilsonian doctrine of self-determination for ethno-religious majorities gave further credence for Nationalists who equated the state with Turks and Muslims. While it is not entirely clear to what degree Turkist political thinking influenced Mustafa Kemal before 1918, one may say with great certitude that the War of Independence, and his ascendency as leader of the National Movement, greatly impacted his perceptions of Turkey as a national home for all Muslim Turks.

The relationship between the old CUP order and the National Movement can be found among other elements of Mustafa Kemal's life during this critical stage of his development. The effort to resist foreign occupation, from the outset of the war, was a Unionist project. CUP loyalists provided the foot soldiers, provisioners, and political leaders that enabled the National Forces from the first days of its existence. The evidence available to us suggests that a consensus within the ranks of the CUP's upper and middle leadership placed Mustafa Kemal in his position as leader of the movement. This consensus was tested over the latter stages of the war, leading to ever-deepening divisions within the Grand National Assembly.

While the CUP may have provided the foundation and the building blocks for the National Movement, it was Mustafa Kemal's mettle as a military and political leader that maintained the coalition's cohesion through the trials of the conflict. The reputation he had cultivated before the war as an independent-minded and competent commander provided him with the opportunity to insert himself among equally reputable and successful military and political figures who staffed the National Forces. While he remained a staunch defender of the state's sovereignty, he betrayed an astute ability to compromise and negotiate between elements of the CUP-turned-Nationalist consensus as well as with representatives of various foreign governments. In prosecuting the war against the Greek expeditionary force, as well as against other invading armies, he capitalized upon the talents of several loyal officers, such as Kazim Karabekir and İsmet İnönü, who bore the brunt of the fighting. In seizing Izmir, he solidified his place within the annals of the empire's history as the last great hero of the Ottoman military. After centuries of successive defeats and humiliation on the battlefield, he secured the Ottoman state one last great victory at the expense of the empire's staunchest adversaries. Within the context of the immediate post-Versailles era, his victory over the Greeks in 1922 possesses an equally profound significance on the global stage. The war transformed Mustafa into a symbol of anti-imperial resistance both within the Ottoman Empire and abroad. For decades to come, Afghans, Iranians, North Africans, South Asians, and many others within the Islamic world would uphold Kemal's Nationalists as models of resistance against Western colonialism.

Despite his new status as a hero in war, Mustafa Kemal's successes came with a political price. Throughout the construction of the National Movement, he had jealously guarded his position of leadership among his peers. His effort to limit or neutralize rival and dissident cliques (such as the Karakol organization and supporters of Enver) led to suspicions early on in his tenure as head of the Defense of Rights Society that Kemal sought power for himself alone. His hold over the office of the presidency of the Grand National Assembly remained less than certain in the months preceding the September 1922 offensive as his rivals began to organize a competing base of power within Ankara. Moreover, the popular rebellions that marked the passage of the War of Independence did not leave him, or the National Movement at large, completely unscarred. While Ankara may have delivered Anatolia from occupation and partition, some urban notables and provincial communities in Asia Minor looked upon the Nationalist Forces as nothing more than a stalking horse for the CUP dictatorship, which had brought grave misfortune to the empire during the preceding decade.

It is clear that Mustafa Kemal understood that the victory he achieved in September 1922 was only the beginning of even greater challenges to come. The expulsion of the Greeks across the Aegean paved the way for further confrontation with Great Britain, whose forces continued to occupy Istanbul and the Dardanelles Straits. Victory over Greece also opened further questions regarding the status of the sultan's government and the future of the Grand National Assembly, a political body that, in principle, was meant to serve as a temporary response to the occupation of the capital. Lastly, the conclusion of the war represented a test for Mustafa's political leadership. As he set aside his role as commander in chief and assumed the duties of a peacetime leader, many of his erstwhile allies sought to carve out their own claims to power. The conclusion of the conflict thus set the stage for a new, and at times violent and divisive, power struggle in Anatolia between the victors of the War of Independence.

| ATATÜRK AS A STATESMAN, |
1923–1927

IN MID-OCTOBER 1922, Refet Pasha, a veteran of World War I and Mustafa Kemal's trusted lieutenant during the latter stage of the War of Independence, disembarked in Istanbul at the head of a small contingent of gendarmes. Refet's visit marked the first time that a high-ranking member of the Nationalist army had entered the Ottoman capital since the fall of Izmir several weeks earlier. Large crowds greeted the general and his men as he undertook several tours of the city. Events since the Greek withdrawal from Anatolia sparked much of the enthusiasm displayed by the city's inhabitants, who lined the docks and streets during Refet's tour of the capital. In the week preceding his arrival, the Ankara government had concluded an armistice with the Allied powers, including Greece. The agreement, which formalized an end of armed hostilities between the Nationalists and Greek forces, outlined a specific framework for Greece's abandonment of Eastern Thrace. While the Nationalist government would have to wait another year for Allied troops to withdraw from Istanbul and the Dardanelles Straits, the signing of the Mudanya Armistice appeared to signal that the recuperation of territory claimed under Ankara's National Pact would proceed without a shot fired in anger by either side.

While enjoying several days of pomp and celebration in various corners of the capital, Refet Pasha's delegation also sought to meet with members of the Istanbul government. Early on in his visit, Refet was granted an audience with Mehmet VI in his palace. The tone of the meeting, by all accounts, was abrupt and coarse. The general, in no uncertain terms, declared to his sovereign that Mustafa Kemal would soon abolish the office of sultan. While Mehmet Vahdeddin had no say in the matter, the Ankara government would allow the monarch to stay on in Istanbul and preside as caliph of Islam. The implication of the Gazi's pronouncement was clear: genuine political power would be divested from Mehmet VI's hands, rendering the sovereign a figurehead at the mercy of the Ankara government.

Victory in the War of Independence, by his own accounting, endowed Mustafa Kemal with a new mandate on political power in what remained of the Ottoman Empire. "Sovereignty," he professed in the fall of 1922, "is acquired by force, by power and by violence." "It was by violence," he added, "that the sons of Osman acquired the power to rule over the Turkish nation. . . . It is now the nation that revolts against these usurpers."[1] In the two years that followed Izmir's fall, Mustafa worked tirelessly to reshape the nature of governance in Anatolia, an enterprise that cemented his position as leader of this revolution. In doing so, he incontrovertibly abolished the lingering vestiges of the Ottoman state, a state he had sworn to serve since he was a youth. The establishment of a republic in the place of an empire was more than just the direct result of the civil conflict encased within the War of Independence. Re-creating governance in Anatolia was equally an expression of the Gazi's own political will to power. As seen from his writings and activities earlier in his career, he had savored those opportunities that allowed him to rise through the ranks of the state. His singular importance within the War of Independence provided him a pretext to realize his boundless political ambitions.

Marginalizing, and eventually eliminating, the sultan proved to be the least of his political challenges in the years immediately following the war. Far graver threats to Mustafa Kemal's standing within postwar Turkey were found among officers and politicians residing in Ankara. Defeating the Greeks and securing Anatolia from partition did not shield him from the criticism of rival representatives within the Grand National Assembly. The loathing and apprehensions harbored within the halls of power in Ankara increasingly extended to Kemal's former close friends and allies who had served alongside him in the National Movement. Individuals such as Rauf Orbay and Kazim Karabekir remained wary of the power the Gazi had accumulated in the waning days of the conflict with Greece. While showing few signs of relinquishing his wartime authority in the aftermath of the Mudanya Armistice, Kemal did little to mend ties with his detractors and erstwhile supporters. In the place of old comrades, he forged a new powerbase among an emerging cadre of allies, men who later became his principal advisors and advocates during the latter stages of his political career. Political tensions between these two factions came to a point of crisis within three years of the republic's christening, resulting in a bloody purge of the old Nationalist regime.

The first years of the Turkish Republic were also a time of profound personal change for Mustafa Kemal Pasha. In the midst of Izmir's destruction, the hero of the War of Independence courted the woman who became his wife. His marriage to Latife represented the culmination of his emotional and, to some degree, political aspirations in love and personal advancement. Yet, as fate would have it, Mustafa's endeavors in marriage proved far less successful than his labors as president of a young republic. Like his relationships with many of his former comrades, personal disagreements and incompatibility gradually undermined Kemal's devotion to Latife.

Diplomacy, as opposed to armed force, captivated much of Mustafa's attention in the weeks immediately following the seizure of Izmir in September 1922. The task of achieving a negotiated settlement with the Allies fell to his loyal lieutenant İsmet

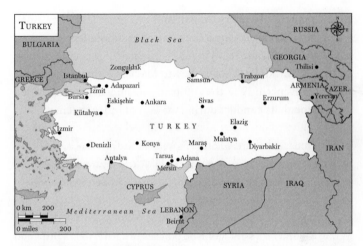

MAP 3. CONTEMPORARY TURKEY

Pasha, who remained in constant contact with Mustafa throughout his meetings with British and Greek representatives at Mudanya. After the signing of the ceasefire in early October, İsmet was again chosen to head Ankara's delegation to the Swiss town of Lausanne, where an international conference settling the Ottoman Empire's political status would open in November. Kemal's reliance upon the hero of the Battle of İnönü as his chief diplomatic representative widened an already substantial gulf between him and other prominent figures in the Nationalist capital. İsmet's ascendency came at the cost of replacing Ankara's foreign minister, Yusuf Kemal, and further marginalizing Rauf Orbay, who had earlier acted as the Ottoman Empire's representative during the negotiation of the Treaty of Brest-Litovsk and the Mondros Ceasefire.

Tensions within the Nationalist camp over diplomatic issues grew more heated in the midst of debate over the future Mehmet VI and the Ottoman sultanate. It is unclear when Mustafa Kemal rendered his decision on abolishing the office of sultan. Despite having long maintained that the War of Independence was fought in the hopes of liberating the sultan from foreign captivity, testimony from his close compatriots, as well as subsequent speeches, suggest that Mustafa had settled on a course of action soon after the Greek withdrawal. According to Mustafa Kemal's own summation of events in 1927, the Ottoman government had impeached itself through its conduct during the War of Independence:

> The Ottoman Empire, whose heirs we were, had no value, no merit, no authority in the eyes of the world. It was regarded as being beyond the pale of international rights and was, as it were, under the tutelage and protection of somebody else.[2]

While Mehmet VI's antagonistic policies toward Ankara provided some initial credence for Refet Pasha's ultimatum to the sultan in mid-October, the Allies' decision to invite a representative from the Istanbul government to talks in Lausanne sealed the Vahdeddin's fate. On October 30, the Grand National Assembly took up legislation abolishing the sultanate. While the bill specified that genuine sovereignty resided in the hands of the Turkish nation, the assembly voted to retain the office of the caliph (a title that would be passed on to the monarch's cousin, Abdülmecid). Over the following months, Mustafa Kemal justified the government's decision to appropriate the sultan's authority on historical grounds. The two offices, in his reading of classical Islamic history, were long separate and were unjustly unified under the rule of the Ottoman household. Even though "sovereign rights belonged to the people" under constitutional rule, he argued before the Grand National Assembly that the caliph would continue to serve as the "conscience and faith of the Islamic world."[3]

In recounting the debate on whether to abolish the sultanate five years later in his 1927 speech, Atatürk claimed that both Rauf Orbay and Refet privately voiced strong sympathies for the sultanate. Both men, Kemal suggested, remained emotionally bound to the Ottoman royal family and the state they represented. While such an anecdote helped to foreshadow his later break with these two former supporters, elite and popular outrage at Ankara's decision to abolish the sultanate did not forestall the assembly's decision. Fearing for his life, Mehmet VI boarded a British ship on the morning of November 17 alongside a large entourage made up of members of his extended family and personal retainers. The ship departed Istanbul and brought the sultan to Malta, where he began an even longer journey as an exiled sovereign. A year and a half after his departure, the Grand National Assembly included Mehmet Vahdeddin among a list of 150 former Ottoman officials and notables who were stripped of their citizenship and declared traitors. The assembly continued to uphold a ban on offering citizenship to the descendants of the Ottoman royal family well after Vahdeddin's death in 1926.

It is during this sensitive and jarring period of Mustafa Kemal's life that the Gazi met his future wife. In the days after the Nationalist entrance into the town, Kemal took up residence in Izmir in the home of Muammer Uşakizade, a prominent local merchant. Muammer's daughter, Latife, had recently returned to Izmir after spending much of her youth studying and traveling in Europe. She, according to accounts of the couple's first encounter, was eager to meet the Gazi, whose exploits she had followed from abroad. Mustafa was impressed with the young woman's character and accomplishments. Fluent in French and English, Latife had studied law in France and possessed cosmopolitan tastes in politics and art. Her affection for him was evident from the outset of her courtship, feelings that Mustafa Kemal returned in kind. His budding relationship with Latife came at the expense of a woman Kemal had romanced during the latter years of the Turkish War of Independence. In 1921, Mustafa's cousin, Fikriye, had come to live with him in Ankara. He became acquainted with the young woman, the daughter of his stepfather's brother, almost twenty years his junior, after his mother fled Salonika for Istanbul. Fikriye entered Mustafa's home as his housekeeper and, according to some accounts, the two developed an amorous relationship over the ensuing months. Like other women who had attracted

Mustafa's attention as a youth, she did possess some education and held progressive views on femininity and politics. After taking up residence in his home, for example, she ceased to wear a head-scarf while in the company of visitors. Nevertheless, the young woman struggled with tuberculosis, which caused her to abandon her studies at a young age. After his initial meeting with Latife, Mustafa encouraged her to seek treatment for her illness abroad in Switzerland, a proposition that Fikriye reluctantly accepted. Once she had left the country, Latife became the Gazi's frequent companion during his tours of the Anatolian countryside.

Scheduled tours and visits to major towns in central and western Anatolia occupied much of Kemal's time during the year following the end of Ankara's war against Greece. In the midst of the intense debates and political jockeying that preoccupied the work of the Grand National Assembly, the Gazi utilized this period to make public appearances, deliver speeches, and address the popular press. The rhetoric and reasoning he employed during discussions and in statements from this period offer valuable insights into how he, as the preeminent figure in postwar Anatolia, intended to lead and shape the state's political future. Before journalists and large crowds, he took great pains to explain his stances on issues related to the abolition of the sultanate and the prospect of permanently moving the seat of government from Istanbul to Ankara (a policy, while not yet enacted, he admitted he had long contemplated). He downplayed the emergence of an oppositional faction in the assembly (the so-called Second Group) and cast further aspersions upon the conduct of CUP officials who had led the Ottoman Empire into World War I. More broadly, he utilized his public appearance as an opportunity to decry and critique those aspects of Ottoman politics and society he found particularly abject and backward. With the war over and the sovereignty of the state appearing increasingly secure, the Turkish people, according to Kemal's reckoning, must now commit themselves to combating a series of threats that had long lingered within the folds of society. Illiteracy, ignorance, and religious superstition had to be defeated or stifled in order for the people and the state to join the community of civilized nations. To remedy these afflictions, profound cultural and political reforms had to be undertaken. The lack of a culture of sport and athletics, for example, was symptomatic of the fact that the Turks of Anatolia had yet to join "the ranks of Europe."[4]

Among the other topics Mustafa Kemal frequently broached during his public tours in the first half of 1923 were the goals and results of the peace talks at the city of Lausanne. İsmet's negotiations with British, Greek, French, and Italian representatives were subject to a great deal of speculation and apprehension in the Ottoman press during this period. Talks between the former warring factions often grew heated, leading to a complete breakdown of discussions between February and April. When negotiations resumed, İsmet's delegation, at Kemal's insistence, stubbornly fought to secure the objectives outlined in the National Pact of 1920. The final peace accord signed between the parties in July 1923 represented the fulfillment of most of the goals set out by the National Movement. The document formally and explicitly recognized Turkey as a politically and economically sovereign state (thus negating the stipulations of the Treaty of Sevrés). Most of the former economic concessions granted by the Ottoman government to various European powers (often referred to as the hated "capitulations") were disavowed or rescinded. Territorially, the Treaty of Lausanne affirmed the inclusion of most of the lands claimed under the National Pact. Among the most contested territorial issues to emerge during negotiations was the status of the old Ottoman province of Mosul, which had been incorporated into the British mandate state of Iraq. Despite İsmet's insistence that the province be included in the Turkish state on economic and ethnic grounds, British negotiators refused to detach the oil-rich province from Baghdad's control. With the two sides at an impasse, a final settlement over the border between Turkey and Iraq was deferred till 1926 when the League of Nations ruled in Great Britain's favor. As in the case of Western Thrace, a region also claimed under the National Pact, Mustafa Kemal assumed a moderate and compromising stance on the question of Mosul's territorial status. The state would gain little in going to war once again for territories that were difficult to defend and retain.

Concluding a peace between Greece and Turkey at Lausanne entailed more than establishing shared borders. Many of the discussions held between the two countries, as well as other affiliated powers, focused on what both Ankara and Athens considered their shared demographic challenges. Despite the decade of conflict

TURKEY'S FIRST FAMILY IN HAPPIER TIMES. *Mustafa Kemal and Latife appear before a crowd.*

that marked relations between the two states, both nations respectively possessed large Orthodox Christian and Muslim minorities. Both sides came to an agreement that past conflicts, as well as the prevailing Wilsonian framework of establishing and solidifying ethnic majorities as the core of the postwar nation-states, made it essential for Turkey and Greece to exchange their corresponding Christian and Muslim populations. Between 1923 and 1924, nearly 500,000 Muslims were evicted from Greece and settled in Anatolia. Ankara, in turn, deported over a million Orthodox Christians from Anatolia. While the Treaty of Lausanne provided specific exemptions for certain portions of the Muslim and Orthodox Christian populations in Greece and Turkey, both governments interpreted the agreement liberally in cleansing their territories of populations deemed nationally or culturally undesirable. Thousands of Turkish-speaking Orthodox Christians who desired to stay in Anatolia were forcibly evacuated to Greece. Similarly, Greece opted to expel thousands of Muslim Albanians to Turkey despite the fact that the treaty had specifically exempted the removal of non-Turkish Muslims. Mustafa Kemal, in his 1927 speech, did not personally address the origins, reasoning, and implications of the population exchange. Yet one of the main negotiators present at Lausanne, Riza Nur, offered this defense of the exchange:

> The most important thing was the liberation of Turkey from the elements which through the centuries had weakened her either by organizing rebellions or by being the domestic extension of foreign states. Hence the making of the country uniformly Turkish ... was a huge and unequalled responsibility. It would have been extremely difficult to make the Greeks agree to this or even to suggest this. Thank God, they were the ones to propose [the exchange of populations].[5]

The arrival of hundreds of thousands of Muslims from Greece in the two years after Lausanne did not conclude Turkey's efforts in engaging with other states seeking to expel their own native Muslim populations. In the decades to come, Ankara formally agreed to accept the arrival of hundreds of thousands of other "undesirable" Muslims from throughout the former Ottoman world.

In expelling the majority of Turkey's Orthodox population, while accepting refugees from the Balkans and the Caucasus, Kemal oversaw the achievement of a political enterprise first initiated by the CUP government at the outset of World War I. Like the Young Turk troika before him, Mustafa saw to it that non-Muslims were marginalized or ceased to exist as a demographic, economic, and political force in Anatolia. Securing the sovereignty state, as well as solidifying the loyal Muslim core of the Ottoman and Turkish nation, demanded, in his eyes, the homogenization of the populace and consolidation of the state's economic resources in the hands of its loyal citizenry. Kemal's effort to "Turkify" Anatolia, beginning with the deportation of native Orthodox Christians, did not progress, however, without long-term complications. While the removal of hundreds of thousands of native Christians entailed the abandonment of vast tracks of land and other property (which was remanded by the state), the nascent Turkish state was forced to contend with the departure of countless professionals and skilled laborers needed to rebuild Anatolia's shattered economy and infrastructure. The effort to develop a stable, healthy, and growing economy was thus hampered over successive decades as the state strove to find and recruit trained and experienced workers capable of physically rebuilding and restoring postwar institutions, industries, and services. Moreover, as seen later in the cases of other postwar imperial states that engaged in the "unmixing" of diverse populations (such as Poland, Bulgaria, Germany, Yugoslavia, and the Soviet Union), the deportation of Greeks left profound cultural and social voids within Turkish society. Discussion and recognition of the communities that were expelled quickly became a taboo within postwar Turkey. Greeks and Armenians, including those who remained, were officially recast as traitors, murders, and collaborators (as opposed to neighbors, friends, or colleagues). Coupled with the abolition of the sultanate, the permanent removal of non-Muslims from Anatolia marked the beginning of a concerted effort to decisively erase Anatolia's Ottoman imperial past.

The signing of the Treaty of Lausanne, which Mustafa Kemal ironically proclaimed was "a peace worthy of our national past," did not soothe tensions within Ankara. İsmet's conduct in Switzerland often had precluded consultation with members of the sitting government (which was then headed by Rauf Orbay), despite disagreement over the procedures and objectives of the negotiations. Meanwhile, in the midst of his tours of the country-side, Kemal had called for a new round of elections, which re-sulted in the formation of a new body of assembly members with even stronger ties to the Gazi. In September, members of the Defense of Rights Society formally renamed their group the Peoples' Party (*Halk Fırkası*) and proclaimed Mustafa Kemal its chairman.

His increasingly consolidated position within Ankara helped to pave the way for the declaration of a republican government in late October 1923. In the weeks and months ahead of the offi-cial announcement, Mustafa had offered hints of this dramatic change to come. In an interview with an Austrian newspaper, he had suggested that the difference between the Ankara govern-ment and the republics of Europe and the Americas was "merely a matter of form."[6] In early October, Ankara was formally declared the country's new capital, a step that ended Istanbul's long-held status as the political epicenter of imperial life (even though the caliph, Abdülmecid, continued to reside in town). Republican rule, in the estimation of Rauf Orbay, Refet, and others, did not neces-sarily entail the expansion of a democratic order but the forma-tion of an even stronger dictatorship in the hands of Mustafa Kemal. Political events from around the world seemed to confirm these suspicions. In Mexico, the restoration of republican rule following a decade of civil war did not deter President Alvaro Obregon, a former general, from governing in a dictatorial manner.

Lenin had also overthrown the age-old imperial system yet continued to govern the Soviet Union with the power and authority of the tsars. It was for this reason that Rauf, in an interview with an Istanbul newspaper, declared that one should not put too much "emphasis on the word 'republic'" since a change in the name of a government would not necessarily "secure the welfare of the nation" or safeguard "the dignity and independence of a country."[7]

Fearing a rising tide of opposition in the National Assembly, Kemal, as president of the body, preemptively dissolved the government and called for the formation of a new cabinet. With the assembly caught off guard and in a state of chaos, Mustafa tabled a resolution to amend the constitution, a proposal supported by allied assemblymen previously briefed on the Gazi's plans. The amendment, which formally declared "the form of government of the Turkish State is a Republic," passed the divided legislature with little debate. News of the adaption of republican rule, which occurred on October 29, caught many of the president's staunchest opponents completely by surprise. Refet Pasha, whose relationship with Kemal had grown strained since the end of war, would learn of the law's passage after a cannon barrage welcoming the decree woke him from his sleep.

The onset of republican governance permanently laid to rest a standing contradiction that defined the state Mustafa Kemal had come to lead. Before October 1923, the state of Turkey had only existed as a name applied to the Anatolian lands contested by the Ottoman government in Istanbul and the Nationalist government of Ankara. Even though the sultan had been removed a year in advance, an act that had affirmed sovereignty upon the "Turkish people," individuals residing in Anatolia legally had remained Ottoman citizens. Establishing a Turkish Republic, in its essence, politically defined all citizens as "Turks" thereafter. This change in the name and nature of government in Anatolia held significant implications for how Ankara would shape the culture and political identity of its citizens. While defining oneself as an Ottoman subject of the sultan may have implied association with different ethnic or sectarian groups, being a Turk in the new republic immediately possessed more narrow connotations. In principle, it signaled an absolute association between the Turkish language and national identity. Moreover, the creation of Turkish citizenship helped to affirm that adherence to Islam, the religion most former Unionists and Nationalists associated with loyal Ottomans, became a defining national trait of the population in the new republic.

The politicking, maneuvering, and travel that occupied much of his time did not completely detract from the attention Mustafa also devoted to his personal life. Shortly after the new year, he asked his aids to assist him in transporting his mother to Izmir. Zübeyde, who was in poor health, arrived by train from Istanbul in January 1923. A large crowd gathered to welcome the Gazi's mother. Latife, who had remained in Izmir while her suitor was away in Ankara, also was present to meet the train and escorted Zübeyde back to her family's home. The relationship between the two women, according to some accounts, was cold from the outset. With her health beginning to fail, Zübeyde betrayed doubts regarding an impending marriage between her son and her new host. Before Mustafa could join his mother, she passed away in late January. Contrary to custom, Kemal did not immediately proceed to Izmir to lay preparations for her burial (choosing instead to attend to political matters in the capital). When the day of her funeral arrived, Mustafa spoke briefly before a small gathering of aides, supporters, and well-wishers. The tone of his funeral address was decidedly political despite the personal loss he suffered. Zübeyde, he explained, suffered greatly in his absence while away at the front during the War of Independence. While he mourned the loss of his mother, he took solace in the political events of the day:

> But there is something that negates my sorrow and consoles me. This something is to know that the administration which brought our mother, the country, to destruction and ruin has gone to the grave of oblivion, never again to return. My mother is under this soil but let national sovereignty last forever.[8]

His choice of words at his mother's graveside reveals much about his personality and frame of mind at this pivotal moment in his life. One could interpret Zübeyde's death as a moment at which Mustafa Kemal distanced himself from his personal past. While her exile from Salonika, as well as the absence of her son, may have pained and embittered her, sapping her health and strength, Mustafa appeared to have consciously detached himself from his past losses and focused upon an emerging divergent future. The weak and duplicitous sultan, at the moment of his funeral speech, was gone and was soon to be replaced by a new republican government, one that was sovereign and strong. While he had served the Ottoman throne and his mother faithfully, the end of the war and the collapse of the empire compelled him to look elsewhere to invest his devotion and passion.

His decision to seek Latife's hand in marriage immediately followed his departure from the cemetery where his mother was laid to rest. The wedding, which occurred two days after the funeral, lacked many of the trappings of a traditional Muslim wedding. After the ceremony, the two departed for Ankara and established a home together in Kemal's mansion in the district of Çankaya. Latife swiftly took to her new role as wife and partner of the country's president. In addition to managing household affairs, she appeared frequently at her husband's side during his tours of the countryside in 1923. Her progressive manner of dress and forceful personality left strong impressions among many who encountered her in the lead-up to the summer elections. Like Halide Edip, a noted feminist and writer who had served as an assistant to Mustafa Kemal during the War of Independence, Latife personified an elite coterie of politically connected women who supported the reformist and iconoclastic policies of the new government. Her rapid ascendency to a position of political and social prominence in 1923 was affirmed during the July elections, when she (like Edip) received token support from voters in Konya for a seat in the Grand National Assembly. In hindsight, she embodied, in appearance and personality, many of the ideals of womanhood later advocated by Mustafa Kemal's government.

As the republic entered its first year, public attention in Ankara and Istanbul turned to discussions in the press regarding the last great political vestige of the Ottoman past: the office of the caliph. Mustafa Kemal, in the aftermath of the sultanate's closure, had initially dispelled any suggestion that his government sought to do away with the caliphate as well. Speaking before journalists in Izmit in January 1923, he pointedly refuted claims that the abolition of the sultanate had damaged the caliph's authority, stating that the caliph had assumed "the most fitting position of authority."[9] By the fall, in the midst of the rumors and discussions in Ankara on the issue of republican government, members of the Istanbul press speculated that Kemal's government was seeking to eliminate Sunni Islam's chief jurist and do away with his powers. A variety of political circles, both inside and outside of Turkey, voiced grave trepidations in both public and private circles. The caliphate, a title which had been acquired by Sultan Selim I in the early sixteenth century, continued to retain profound political and religious significance for many pious and secular Turkish Muslims. In addition to his status as the vicar of all Sunni Muslims, some argued that the caliph was an essential institution in unifying the Turkish nation and sanctifying laws passed by the Grand National Assembly. Many Muslims residing outside of Turkey also professed strong attachments to the caliphate. South Asian Sunni and Shiite activists, for example, played especially vocal roles in supporting the National Movement in British India, calling for greater solidarity among Muslims around the world in support of Mustafa Kemal's struggle to liberate the caliph from foreign occupation. Ankara's decision to abolish the Ottoman sultanate and establish the Turkish Republic in its place, in the eyes of many prominent South Asian supporters, signaled an alarming turn in their struggle to preserve the caliph as a symbol of international Muslim unity against Western imperialism.

In November 1923, two outspoken members of Indian's pro-caliphate movement posted a pleading letter to İsmet, who was then serving as Mustafa Kemal's prime minister, decrying "the uncertain position of the Caliph-Imam." For the sake of maintaining the "religious and moral solidarity of Islam," the caliph's position had to be secured.[10] Elements within the Istanbul press shared this sentiment. "To endanger the Caliphate," in the words of one editor, "the heritage of the Ottoman dynasty acquired forever by Turkey, would apparently be an action which could by no means be in accord with reason, patriotism or national sentiment."[11]

The intervention of noted South Asian Islamists into the caliphate debate served to strengthen, rather than weaken, the consensus of forces within the Grand National Assembly against the caliph. The letter, in the eyes of several ranking members of the Peoples' Party, did not represent a sincere effort by pious Muslims but a British plot to undermine Turkish sovereignty. Unlike the debates that had preceded the establishment of the republic, Kemal assumed a far more muted position in discussions on this issue in the winter of 1924. Formal debate in the Ankara legislature on the caliphate's status soon followed the February publication of an editorial in a pro-government daily declaring the office of the caliph an institution incapable of reconciling itself with the democratic order of the republic. Before the Grand National Assembly, one deputy suggested that Islamic law and jurisprudence did not mandate the need of a caliph and that it was secular political leaders who historically had created and upheld the office on the basis of their own personal prerogatives and legitimacy. When İsmet rose to speak, he dispensed with the dogmatic and religious contours of the debate. For the hero of the Battle of İnönü, the caliphate debate provided another opportunity to underscore the difference between the republican government and the ancient regime. The sultan/caliph, he reminded the assembly, had supported the CUP's costly decision to side with Germany, which threw the nation "into the horror of the general war".[12] Retaining the caliphate, he maintained, clashed with Ankara's prerogatives since Mehmet VI, as caliph, had supported the fatwa condemning Mustafa Kemal and the National Forces as rebels. Doing away with the institution was therefore necessary to correct the wrongs of the past. İsmet's invocations of the past were at odds with realities of the caliph's role in the wars that ended the Ottoman Empire. Prominent members of the CUP, including İsmet, had supported the sultan/caliph's religious justification for joining World War I. More to the point, İsmet and his fellow Nationalists had never advanced any ill will or antipathy toward the sultan/caliph during their struggle for independence; to the contrary, the future sovereignty of the state, according to many within the Defense of Rights Society, depended upon the restoration of the caliph as an integral component of a postwar state. These contradictions, however, were not mentioned in the course of the caliphate debate.

Debate in the Grand National Assembly came to an end in the first week of March 1924 with passage of a law entailing the abolition of the caliphate and the expulsion of the remainder of the Ottoman royal family. During the same legislative session, assembly members abruptly instituted several additional, even more drastic bills with regard to the role religious officials were to play in republican politics. This additional set of laws mandated the closure of the official religious school system and the creation a single, unified public education system governed from Ankara. They also entailed the abolition of the office of the *şeyülislam* and the closure of Ottoman ministries that managed pious foundations (*vakifs*) and other religious activities. In the place of these imperial offices, the assembly laid the foundation for a new Ministry of Religious Affairs, a department which, as the constitution would later stipulate, would "execute the works concerning the beliefs, worship, and ethics of Islam, enlighten the public about their religion, and administer the sacred worshipping places."[13] The assembly further augmented these laws a month later with the passage of legislation outlawing the Ottoman religious court system which judged civil cases based upon Islamic jurisprudence.

A Vehicle for Radical Change. *A full session of the Turkish Grand National Assembly soon after independence.*

Mustafa Kemal did not begin to speak publically on the question of caliphate and the role of Islam in Turkish society until after Abdülmecid II and his family had departed the old capital. The caliphate, he explained to one foreign reporter, "was a thing of the past" and had no place in contemporary times.[14] He categorically rejected calls from abroad that he, as president of the Turkish Republic, should assume the title of caliph for himself. Those who "occupy themselves with the chimera of the Caliphate and thereby mislead the Muslim world" were, from his perspective in 1927, "the enemies of the Muslim world" and Turkey in particular.[15]

A separate line of reasoning governed Mustafa Kemal's views on the elimination of former Ottoman religious institutions and offices. Various personal writings and statements from the pre-republican era suggest that he had long harbored strong anticlerical proclivities. He repeatedly castigated Islamic teachers and scholars as the propagators of ignorance and reaction in the Ottoman lands. Saving the state, and preserving its sovereignty, required the cultivation of an educational and philosophical framework free, or relatively exclusive, of Islamic precepts. In excluding clerics from the judiciary, Kemal liberated the state from the need to reconcile future legal reforms with religious dogmas. On the face of it, the secularization and nationalization of the Turkish legal and educational system corresponded with the reformatory trends seen in Europe and the rest of the "civilized world" at large.

Mustafa would never deny that Islam was at the core of Turkish identity. According to the first draft of the Turkish constitution in 1924, the Grand National Assembly categorically stipulated that Islam was the official religion of the Turkish state (a stipulation that remained enshrined in constitutional law until 1937). Nevertheless, in recognizing Islam as a force binding the republic citizens together culturally, morally, and historically, his supporters in the Grand National Assembly sought to integrate religious scholars and preachers into the broader enterprise of building and maintaining the Turkish Republic. Ankara's new Ministry of Religious Affairs formally transformed the country's Islamic clergy into state employees, thereby placing homilies and religious instruction under official oversight. The government's appropriation of Islamic expression and activism, it was hoped, would allow state officials to monitor and further harness the passions and loyalty of the Turkish populace and, in the long run, direct the population toward more modern and civilized modes of behavior and belief.

While many politicians in Ankara sympathized with the government's plans to secularize and reform Islam's place in Turkish society, a number of dissidents inside and outside of the assembly interpreted the displacement of the caliphate as yet another signal pointing to the establishment of a dictatorship under Mustafa Kemal. In hindsight at least, Kemal did acknowledge that elements of the press, as well as his own party, feared the direction in which he was taking the Turkish government. During his 1927 speech, the Gazi took note of editorials that struck subtle comparisons between the new republican government in Turkey and the authoritarian republics emerging elsewhere in the world. He specifically cited the case of an editorial that drew parallels between the republic government in the Americas versus the republicanism in Turkey. There was very little difference between republicanism and absolutism in the Americas, the paper warned. Typically, those military leaders who "become President of the Republic by force" tend to take "the place of a hereditary monarch."[16] Kemal dismissed such criticism as misguided. As he would explain toward the end of his lengthy *Nutuk*, he began to suspect by the summer of 1924 that such expressions of opposition helped to shed light on the state's true enemies. This accusation, levied in 1927, centered on the formation of the first, and only, genuine opposition party established during the early republican era.

The establishment of a second political party in Turkey was an issue of intense debate among former CUP officials since the first days of the post-armistice era. Before the summer elections of 1923, some had contemplated the reconstitution of the Committee of Union and Progress (Mustafa Kemal, according to some sources, knew and approved of such discussions). By the following summer, plans were set in motion for the creation of an entirely new party, one that explicitly countered the authoritarian tendencies of the governing Peoples' Party. In November 1924, a slew of formerly prominent Nationalist officials and officers resigned their posts in the government and established the Progressive Republican Party (PRP). Rauf Orbay, Kazim Karabekir, Refet, and Ali Fuat, each a former close comrade and lieutenant of Mustafa Kemal, publicly joined the party. Kemal, as he later explained in 1927, had anticipated the gathering of these opponents. The marshaling of these forces, he suspected, represented the formation of a conspiracy bent upon overthrowing his person. It is for this reason that he demanded in October 1923 that all elected officials holding commissions in the Turkish Army resign from their posts in the Grand National Assembly. With this step, as he later explained, dissidents conspiring against him in the legislature would be forced to choose between civilian life (detached from the army) or serve loyally as officers in the nation's military.

Mustafa's personal insecurity within the halls of the Grand National Assembly mirrored his increasingly troubled life at home. Despite their public displays of camaraderie, relations between Kemal and Latife turned sour during their first year of marriage. Many of the president's contemporaries describe his wife as a forceful figure who attempted to manage and supervise her husband's social interactions. Mustafa, a man who had long enjoyed carousing and socializing into the wee hours of the morning, bridled under his wife's admonitions. His fondness for alcohol, which he often drank to excess, was purportedly a frequent matter of conflict between the two. Their marriage grew further strained when Fikriye, Mustafa Kemal's former lover, arrived in Ankara in the summer of 1924. Fikriye had cut short her treatment for tuberculosis in Europe after having learned of Kemal's marriage. Despite efforts to prevent her from visiting the capital, in June she arrived unannounced in Ankara at the president's mansion. Attendants intercepted her at the gates of the house, forcing her to leave by carriage. As the wagon pulled away, Fikriye produced a gun and shot herself. Neither Mustafa Kemal nor Latife made any formal comment on Fikriye's suicide. Nevertheless, as events would later unfold, the death of his former lover served to hasten the dissolution of Kemal's marriage.

As Turkey entered the winter of 1925, developments outside of Ankara stoked still further anxieties and tension. The abolition of the caliphate, as well as the imposition of new constrains and prohibitions on Islamic institutions, did not pass unnoticed by elements of the country's provincial communities. A handful of public disturbances in various corners of Anatolia signaled, to some degree, initial public discontent with the radical reforms imposed by the capital. Still deeper sources of discontent with the revolutionary changes in Ankara sparked more violent demonstrations of popular outrage in eastern Anatolia. Fighting broke out in the distant province of Hakkari in the fall of 1924 between Turkish

military units and rebels drawn from the region's Nestorian population, resulting in a wave of mass deportations targeting this small
eastern Christian community. An even larger revolt erupted in
February 1925 when insurgents clashed with local gendarmerie
units outside a village near the town of Diyarbakir. The leader of
the rebels, Sait of Palu, was a Kurdish sheikh (or holy man) who
commanded the loyalty of a local spiritual order of Nakshibandi
mystics. Sheikh Sait, in sounding the call to rebel, appealed to all
Muslims in the Turkish Republic to rise up and depose the government's godless handlers. His followers made quick territorial
gains in the environs of Diyarbakir over the first month of the
revolt, eventually laying siege to the town itself. The outbreak
and sudden successes of the insurrection caught Mustafa Kemal's
government by complete surprise. At great financial cost, the
Grand National Assembly authorized the mobilization of a large
force to march on Diyarbakir and suppress Sait's rebels. The fighting subsided in April with Sait's capture.

The confluence of factors leading to the Sheikh Sait rebellion
speaks to the various degrees to which many Kurds living in
portions of the Turkey's southeastern provinces greeted the early
republican era with apprehension and outrage. During the course
of the War of Independence, Mustafa Kemal was vocal in his recognition of Kurdish interests and support for the Nationalist
cause. He repeatedly declared that Kurdish and Turkish devotion
to Islam and the Ottoman state bound them together as brothers
in arms and fellow citizens. Immediately after the war, he acknowledged that the state did possess dense Kurdish populations
in "very limited areas" and that it would perhaps be necessary to
allow certain Kurdish-speaking counties to govern themselves
autonomously "in accordance with our constitution."[17] However,
when the Grand National Assembly met in 1924 to finalize the
republic's constitution, assembly members refused to implement
any framework for provincial autonomy in any portion of Turkey.
Anger among Kurdish notables at Mustafa Kemal's refusal to
uphold his wartime pledges to his Kurdish supporters amplified

popular rage toward with the assembly's collective decision to abolish the caliphate and outlaw autonomous religious schools and endowments. The indignation that coaxed the peasant followers of the Sheikh Sait to rise up was likewise the product of new taxes and the appointment of new local officials from outside of southeastern Turkey. While the rebellion did attract the support and involvement of intellectuals and former Ottoman officers who desired the creation of an independent Kurdish state, recent studies of Sheikh Sait's insurrection suggest that more immediate, provincial concerns compelled most rebels to take up arms.

Neither Mustafa Kemal nor the Grand National Assembly at large interpreted the revolt as a limited or isolated affair. "Reactionary" uprisings had early gripped the eastern regions of Dersim and Hakkari, movements that not only represented rejections of Ankara's authority but also bore the hallmarks of foreign interference (since British agents were suspected of fomenting revolt in areas close to the borders of Iraq). Under Kemal's direction, the government took up a bill placed before the Grand National Assembly giving the state inordinate powers of authority. The Maintenance of Order Law, enacted in March 1925, gave the government authority to ban all publications and organizations deemed officially subversive. The assembly also approved steps calling for the creation of two "Independence Tribunals" tasked with prosecuting individuals suspected of fomenting rebellions. It was under the auspices of the Independence Tribunal in Diyarbakir that Sheikh Sait was found guilty of treason and publically executed in June 1925.

Testimony from one of Sait's former supporters cast the rebellion in a new light by the summer of 1925. The witness, a relative of a prominent Kurdish nationalist and key organizer of the insurrection, suggested that the rebels had hoped that the Progressive Republican Party would eventually support the creation of an independent Kurdistan. Mustafa Kemal and his allies in the Grand National Assembly seized upon this statement as further evidence of a conspiracy to overthrow the government.

On June 3, the government officially banned the PRP, stating that the party's bylaws, which explicitly mentioned support for personal religious beliefs, had encouraged those Islamic reactionaries who had fomented the uprising. Mustafa Kemal, in 1927, reiterated his belief that the PRP's support for individual religious beliefs encouraged and harbored the insurgents, stating the opposition's use of the terms "progress" and "republic" was meant to mask "the flag of religion from our sight." Through this ruse, the PRP allied themselves with "people who are in our country as well as abroad" seeking to devise "all sorts of plots with the purpose of raising . . . a general rebellion."[18]

In the twelve months that followed the death of Sheikh Sait and the closure of the PRP, Mustafa Kemal intensified his efforts to rein in other reactionary forms of religious and ethnic expression. Citing the role played by Sait's Nakshibandi order in organizing the Kurdish revolt, the Independence Tribunal ordered the closure of mystical Sufi lodges throughout eastern Anatolia. The Grand National Assembly, in November 1925, affirmed the court's decision and further demanded that all Islamic fraternal orders, as well as popular shrines, be disbanded or closed. Days before approving this measure, the assembly also passed a law outlawing the wearing of turbans and fezzes, the traditional headwear most favored by conservative or pious Muslims. In the place of these past symbols of Ottoman culture and status, Mustafa Kemal personally encouraged Turkish men to adopt more "civilized" or "modern" headgear with brims. The initiation of this law, as Kemal later explained in his *Nutuk*, bore direct implications over the future of the republic:

> It was necessary to abolish the fez, which sat on our heads of ignorance, fanaticism, of hatred to progress and civilization, and to adopt in its place the hat, the customary headdress of the whole civilized world, thus showing among other things, that no difference existed in the manner of thought between the Turkish nation and the whole family of civilized mankind.[19]

Other expressions of traditional, particularly Islamic, culture came under the preview of government reform and intervention between the fall of 1925 and 1926. The Islamic calendar (which marked Mohammed's flight to Medina in 622 as the beginning of the common era) was officially disowned in favor of the Gregorian calendar. Between February and March 1926, the assembly adopted a gamut of new civil and criminal legal codes based upon Swiss and Italian statutes. In the absence of the Ottoman court system, this new juridical framework provided a concrete system that finalized the elimination of traditional Islamic precedents covering such personal matters of inheritance, marriage, and divorce. The new statutes particularly represented a dramatic shift in the government's recognition of women's rights. While women remained disenfranchised from the right to vote, the 1926 reforms abolished legal barriers prohibiting women from working and traveling and afforded them greater rights to marry, separate from their husbands, and inherit assets from deceased family members.

This onslaught levied against various facets of traditional Islamic practices and precedents embodied two principal facets that had come to define Mustafa Kemal's earlier years as president of the Turkish Republic. On the one hand, it represented a continuation of his effort to void elements of the Ottoman governance and culture. His repudiation of religious precepts found in the state's legal code, as well as within Anatolian society at large, certainly reflected his own strong secular sympathies and preferences. Turkey's new and emerging civic culture, he would repeatedly claim, was in keeping with broader global trends. The formation of a modern civilized society demanded aggressive steps to combat sources of ignorance and religious dogma that sullied the nation. Yet in the context of the postwar era, Ankara's budding cultural revolution represented a protracted campaign to delegitimize and eradicate the political vestiges of the empire the republic had replaced. Mustafa Kemal, as well as others around him, equated the power of religious figures, as well as the Islamic culture such individuals upheld, with the sultanate and empire that had impugned itself during the War of Independence. To a certain degree, the adoption of new legal codes and the prohibitions placed upon the men's headwear represented an extension of Mustafa Kemal's post-1920 efforts to define Ankara as a distinct and legitimate source of political and civic leadership.

On the other hand, the sweeping reforms undertaken in the aftermath of the Sheikh Sait Rebellion possessed more immediate and fundamental implications for Kemal's government. The insurrection, coupled with the formation of the PRP, underscored the relative delicacy of the president's hold on power. The extent to which the Gazi's allies in the Grand National Assembly feared the emergence of the PRP was fundamentally manifested in the decision by the governing party to formally change their name to the Republican Peoples' Party (lest the opposition claim a mandate in representing the state's republican interests). Sheikh Sait's demise, as well as suggestions that Kurdish separatists favored Kemal's opponents, offered the government an opportunity to take the offensive against any and all centers of political dissent. Asserting the supremacy of the Republican Peoples' Party (RPP) and its hold over power ultimately entailed more than crushing the PRP or executing a handful of rebels. The reforms struck at the core of provincial society, targeting both groups and potential symbols that could foment popular revolt. The sheer act of demanding new codes of conduct and civil engagement accentuated Ankara's desire to extract the loyalty and service of each citizen in the Turkish Republic. The outbreak of further, albeit smaller, acts of rebellion in response to the hat law of 1925, from the perspective of Mustafa Kemal and others in the capital, served to sustain the government's propagation of the Maintenance of Order Law. Authoritarian governance, in other words, could not be decoupled from social or political reform; both served the interest of maintaining a strong, sovereign, and independent state.

Political tensions in the countryside and infighting in the capital took a toll on Mustafa Kemal's health during his first years in office. In the midst of the government negotiations on the status of the caliphate, he had suffered from severe chest pains. Doctors quickly rushed to his bedside and deduced that the president was suffering from angina. Despite having suffered an earlier cardiac episode during the course of the War of Independence, Kemal continued to smoke and drink heavily both before and after falling ill in November 1924. He also continued to maintain a rigid regime of travel throughout this period. Between 1924 and 1926, the Gazi undertook several extended tours of the Anatolian countryside, visiting newly opened schools and delivering lengthy public speeches before crowds of cheering supporters.

It was during one of his tours in August 1925 that Mustafa formally ended his marriage to Latife. The two, according to those who knew the couple intimately during their brief life together, had grown increasingly estranged from one another during the course of troubled months leading up to the Sheikh Sait Rebellion. Latife had continued to voice her displeasure with her husband's carousing and late-night social engagements both at home and while traveling the countryside. Mustafa equally admonished his wife for interfering in his personal life and choice of friends. Ironically, their divorce occurred months in advance of the government's decision to alter the country's marriage laws. Mustafa informed his wife of their formal separation by mail, a right reserved to men under Islamic precedent. With little choice in the matter, Latife purportedly attempted to salvage the relationship but was refused any audience with her husband. Over the following years, she resumed a quiet life living in Istanbul and refused to comment publicly on her failed marriage to the founder of the Republic of Turkey (to this day, her descendants have resisted calls to publish her personal papers from this period).

The personal repercussions of Mustafa Kemal's divorce appeared to not have deterred or distracted him from his political duties during the course of 1926. He continued to tour central and western Anatolia between the spring and summer of that year. In mid-June, he arrived in the northwestern town of Balikesir with the intention of spending the night before proceeding on to Izmir later in the week. Late in the evening on June 15, a man appeared before the governor of Izmir with urgent news pertaining to the president. The man, an immigrant from Crete by the name of Şevki, informed the governor that he knew of a plot against the Gazi. Local authorities responded to the man's accusations by arresting four men. One of the men arrested was Ziya Hurşit, a former assembly member elected from a district located on Turkey's northeastern coast. Hurşit, upon his apprehension, produced bombs that he confessed would have been used to kill Mustafa Kemal.

A political firestorm ensued in the days immediately following official disclosure of the supposed Izmir conspiracy. An Independence Tribunal, similar to the ones established to investigate and prosecute the Sheikh Sait Rebellion, was soon established in Izmir. While under questioning in police custody, Ziya Hurşit claimed that the plot had been hatched a year in advance and that many of the conspirators were former members of the Progressive Republican Party. Within a matter of days, government authorities executed a dragnet targeting a wide range of erstwhile political opponents of Mustafa Kemal. The initial list of suspects sought on suspicion of complicity in the Izmir conspiracy included the names of many of the country's most prominent citizens: Rauf Orbay, Kazim Karabekir, Refet, Ali Fuat, and many others. Before the Independence Tribunal of Izmir, which began its proceedings on June 18, Ziya Hurşit and his fellow conspirators apprehended in Izmir contradicted one another on whether the Progressive Republican Party had endorsed or sought to profit from the slaying of Mustafa Kemal. State prosecutors, despite these contradictions, insisted that the party's leadership, as a whole, conspired against the president. The goal, according to the state's inquisitor, Necip Ali, was to re-establish the Committee of Union and Progress, a party which he portrayed as the source of the nation's troubles beginning with World War I. In mid-July, the judge issued guilty verdicts for fifteen individuals accused of overthrowing the constitution and the Grand National Assembly. All fifteen were executed later that evening. Among those who met an untimely end as a result of the trial were Ziya Hurşit, his fellow assassins, and such prominent wartime figures as Ismail Canbolat, one-time governor of Istanbul and republican minister. Kara Kemal, cofounder of the Karakol organization, was condemned to death in absentia and committed suicide upon his discovery by police in late July.

Other notable figures indicted by the Izmir court were released following the closure of the tribunal in July. Mustafa Kemal, who grew concerned over the effect the Izmir trials had upon popular opinion and the loyalty of the military, was instrumental in convincing members of the tribunal to dismiss the charges levied against Kazim Karabekir, Ali Fuat, and Refet. Others, namely Rauf Orbay, were not as lucky. While the court had cleared him and several other prominent PRP members of any direct involvement in the Izmir plot, a new Independence Tribunal was convened in Ankara in August with the intention of prosecuting all those who stood to gain politically from the attempt on the president's life. The Ankara trial, which lasted three weeks in total, was composed of a series of interrogations of former CUP officials who had been politically active in the War of Independence and the first years of the Turkish Republic. Witness testimony, as extracted by the prosecution, constituted a tutorial on the incompetence of the CUP high command during World War I and the duplicitous dealings of Kemal's political opponents (particularly those who had supported Enver Pasha). Very little of the testimony presented before the court implicated the key figures on trial of the charges of resurrecting Unionism. On October 26, the court condemned four men to hang. Rauf Orbay, who had exiled himself to Europe before the opening of the Izmir trials, was found guilty of inciting the murder of the Gazi and was sentenced to ten years in prison.

When Mustafa Kemal took the stage before the second annual congress of the Republican Peoples' Party in October 1927, the

THE GAZI'S WOULD-BE ASSASSINS. *Two defendants, Yusuf and Ismail, appear in court soon after their arrest in the infamous "Izmir Plot."*

consequences of the Izmir and Ankara trials remained a topic of heated debate and sensitivity. In concluding his thirty-six-hour *Nutuk*, he rendered an absolute and unforgiving interpretation of the political events that had preceded the formation of the tribunals and the conviction of so many eminent figures associated with the foundation of the republic. The government's actions, which included the imposition of martial law and the acquisition of other arbitrary powers by the Grand National Assembly, had saved the state from disorder and "put an end to the injurious organization which bore the name 'Republican Progressive Party.'" "The avenging hand of Republican justice" required harsh measures in order to suppress an "army of conspirators."[20] With the state's security and sovereignty restored, all powers conferred upon the government through the Maintenance of Order Law would be rescinded. Time would show, he argued, that the powers invested in him, as president, did not transform him into a dictator or despot during this crisis.

At the moment he ended his 1927 speech, Mustafa was a man who possessed peerless political authority and influence in Ankara. His *Nutuk*, with its many indictments, criticisms, tributes, and declarations, is a lasting testament to the power he had acquired by this moment in his life. While some of his statements and speeches predating the RPP second congress did allude to how he imagined himself within Turkey's fight for independence, the speech of 1927 sounded a final chord on where Kemal stood within the country's grand narrative. His struggles, trials, and victories, according to his own reading of the immediate past, were one and the same as those experienced by the country and its citizens. Turkey's genesis came at great physical and emotional cost and entailed confrontation with enemies and traitors both foreign and domestic. Mustafa Kemal's many denunciations in the speech implicated both staunch foes as well as former comrades and close friends, thus making it clear that the nation's pain and conflicts resounded in his own life. He finished the *Nutuk* leaving no doubt that history had already passed its judgment on him and the state he created. The nation's independence was, in his own words, "a holy treasure," and he alone had laid it "in the hands of the youth of Turkey."[21]

Naturally, Kemal's 1927 reconstruction of his rise to power and prominence is not free of irony or contradiction. The conspirators he castigated with such vigor through the latter portions of his speech were men who were his political equals or superiors at the start of the Turkish War of Independence. All of those blamed for the conspiracy in Izmir, as well as those who charged them, were at one point or another loyal Young Turks. In recounting his actions from 1922 forward, he repeatedly maligned those who feared or criticized the autocratic policies of his party and government. National elections, as well as victory in war, had provided him and his supporters a justifiable mandate to govern in spite of those who opposed him inside and outside the capital. Dissent, as he perceived it, was the work of the reactionaries or worse.

Critical to understanding Mustafa Kemal's reasoning and behavior during the four years following the Mudanya Armistice (as depicted in the *Nutuk* and elsewhere) is his rendering of the ends and ambitions he coveted with the fulfillment of the National Movement. While he admittedly had long sought greater authority and political status for himself, it is clear that Kemal did not savor power for its own sake. Time and again, he professed an unwavering belief in his abilities to "save the state" and reset its foundations as a member of the "family of civilized nations." In saving the state, he betrayed a common conviction found among many Young Turk officers of his generation: in his estimation, all sources of political contention and regression had to be confronted, bested, and, if need be, replaced or eradicated. The sultan and caliph, as individuals and as institutions, had demonstratively undermined the state's independence during the darkest hours of the National Movement. Therefore, with the conflict over, Kemal placed an imperative upon eliminating all remnants of those bastions of treason associated with the Ottoman state.

Displacing the sultanate, the caliphate and the empire's Islamic legal system represented complementary efforts in consolidating power and ensuring the sovereignty and rationality of the Kemalist state. Time and again, the Gazi and his most loyal supporters underscored the need to liberate the republic from the control from foreign and reactionary sources of influence and authority. While he had curried favor early on with Muslim revolutionary and activists from South Asia, Russia, and North Africa before his victory over the Greeks, Mustafa Kemal remained adamant that his administration was not beholden to the desires and demands of the Islamic world. Moreover, securing the republic and maintaining its independence necessitated radical changes to the mores and institutions that condemned Ottoman Anatolian society to occupation, violence, and humiliation in the first place. Advancing a stringently secular agenda was not simply a matter of changing one's tastes and values for the sake of progress; in Kemal's estimation, Islam was to be banished from public forums of expression and representation because it was integral to an imperial culture that had corroded or limited the government's ability to act rationally and effectively.

A further, and more divisive, test of his resolve as the leader of a fledgling state was manifested among his former allies and supporters (including individuals who were once personally tied to Mustafa Kemal). Beginning with the War of Independence, Kemal revealed himself to be a man with an obstinate will in the face of adversity. Achieving the seemingly unachievable goal of restoring the state's sovereignty and dignity despite war and occupation was attained despite his detractors in the National Assembly and in the Anatolian countryside. His decision to meet his political opponents with violence and oppression after the war's end echoes the bloody impact the conflict had upon him and those around him. Statehood, he posed during the closing stages of his *Nutuk*, came at "the price of streams of blood which have drenched every foot of our beloved homeland."[22] Maintaining the state's independence and sovereignty into the future required similar costs to be paid. In the place of those individuals and voices deemed expendable or untrustworthy (such as Rauf, Kazim, and Ali Fuat), Mustafa found more willing (and at times quite sycophantic) retainers he could entrust to carry out his orders and fulfill his vision for the future (İsmet İnönü, despite some periods of mutual tension, does to some degree fit this description).

Kemal's brief marriage to Latife exemplified both the costs and limits of his political evolution during these impactful years. The forging of their relationship complemented their mutual personalities and ambitions. Latife, as a sophisticated, independent, and progressive woman from a wealthy trading family, bore a strong resemblance to many of the women he had fancied and romanced in the past. She, in courting the favor of the country's founder and greatest hero, graciously and willingly accepted her role as the president's spouse. Elements of both the press and the public accepted her as a new ideal of womanhood and Turkish citizenship, a status not lost upon the two of them. Yet it is clear that Mustafa's work habits and personal behavior taxed their relationship. His wife's efforts to engage his attention and tame his socializing and drinking, by all accounts, entailed concessions he was not willing to accept. Their divorce, from the perspective of those who knew them both, was a reflection of the obstinate, detached, and independent disposition he displayed in politics. Like many of those he bested or marginalized in politics, Latife ultimately accepted her dispossession and withdrew from the public limelight out of deference to the Gazi.

As Mustafa Kemal's steadily solidified his political standing within the young republic in the years between 1922 and 1927, the content of his statesmanship was only beginning to unfold. Unseating the sultan/caliph and establishing a robust government under the control of his Republican Peoples' Party, by his own accounting, were in the service of a grander enterprise. These early reforms represented a bridgehead paving the way for more elemental changes to be thrust upon the Turkish nation. Joining the family of civilized nations required the establishment of a strong state worthy of international respect as well as a culture and an economy rooted in new globally accepted modern norms. While the policies he would propagate over the course of his presidency were set in opposition to the Ottoman past, Mustafa Kemal's drive to transform Anatolian politics, economy, and culture was in impulse rooted in his imperial education and service. By the time of his death in 1938, the Republic of Turkey simultaneously embodied new standards and customs, as well as past aspirations, in keeping with Anatolia's complex and tortured modern history.

CHAPTER 5

| ATATÜRK AS AN ICON, |
| 1927–1938 |

THERE ARE A NUMBER OF STORIES found in memoirs and biographies that are used to exemplify Mustafa Kemal's achievements and charisma. Collectively, many of these incidents unfold like morality tales and fables in which Atatürk plays the role of a teacher, mentor, or visionary. One such story, as recounted by journalist Ahmet Emin Yalman, concerns a visit the president took in 1925 to the provincial town of Kastamonu. The town, as Yalman explained, enjoyed a reputation for religious conservatism. Before an assembly of local residents, the Gazi unveiled a collection of hats with brims, which he distributed among the crowd as gifts. Many religious conservatives in the audience were dismayed at the gesture, disparaging the "Western" hat as an inherently un-Islamic innovation. Kemal met these criticisms forcefully, arguing that the Ottoman government had introduced the fez to the public many years earlier. Since the fez replaced the turban, an even older Islamic piece of headgear, as an article of clothing favored by Muslims of all walks of life, only prejudice and ignorance now prevented people from accepting the hat as a new mode of fashion regardless of one's piety. Moved by the president's words, the conservatives in the crowd ultimately led a parade through the center of town, with each man wearing a hat with a brim. The moral of the story, in Yalman's words, was clear: even "the conservative men of Kastamonu," the most pious men of the nation, could not deny the Gazi's leadership, eloquence, and reasoning.[1]

Such stories are not simply the product of contemporary mythmaking. Mustafa Kemal, particularly during the final decade of his life, savored the opportunity to promote himself as a man whose fame and abilities exceeded his accomplishments on the battlefield. Even before the conclusion of the Izmir trial, which marked Kemal's unrivaled ascendency within the Turkish Republic, he steadily embraced a number of new roles and personas in the public domain. He regularly presented himself as the country's premiere educator whose lessons were meant to uplift and fundamentally transform the nation. He equally fancied himself a thinker and scholar. By the end of his life, there was seemingly no topic that had not received a modicum of his interest or elicited at least some opinion. Above all, Mustafa Kemal portrayed himself as a father and model of the Turkish nation. Both at home and abroad, he consciously exploited his past and present feats as the basis for his paternal relationship to his young state. His governing philosophy, as well as his tastes and personal conduct, served as the primary basis of being a Turk. By the time of his death, his principles assumed almost liturgical qualities in the eyes of his retainers and supporters. Foreign observers and commentators further inflated Atatürk's Nietzschean stature. In the context of the interwar period, international commentators elevated him into a man who was equal to, or perhaps surpassed, the new standards of enlightened autocratic leadership founded in the Western and non-Western world.

The cultivation of these various personas reflected more than Mustafa Kemal's deep-seated drive to attain political power. It is clear that he propagated his public image as a leader with manifold abilities and qualities as a means to execute a wide series of agendas and policies meant to secure Turkey's independence and strength beyond the limits of his tenure as president. Establishing a "New Turkey" entailed both a revolution in the structure of government as well as a transformation of the society that buttressed the state. Transforming the content of the Turkish national character was a project designed to eliminate or suppress those aspects of Anatolian society that he deemed the root causes of the political, economic, and social degeneration that had plagued the Ottoman state and nearly strangled the Turkish Republic in its infancy. He took great pride in introducing (or perhaps reintroducing) Turkey to the global community of nations as a modern, civilized state worthy of international esteem. While one may be able to trace the intellectual and personal impulses he exhibited as president to his earlier education and experiences as an Ottoman officer, his foreign admirers and native supporters portrayed him as a man possessing a distinctively unrivaled vision. His exceptional and solitary public persona as the leader of the Turkish nation resonated in his personal life. As an unmarried man, he kept few close companions. While Mustafa Kemal did beget a family of eight adopted children in the latter years of his life, only

TURKEY'S FATHER ARRIVES. *Mustafa Kemal Atatürk disembarks from a train on one of his many tours of the country.*

a few enjoyed a close relationship with their father. The rigors of his political duties and activities, as well as fondness for drink, reflected the apparent loneliness of his final years and helped to hasten his physical demise.

The last decade of Mustafa's life lacked much of the drama and heated tempo of the earlier years that defined his rise to power. The suppression of the Progressive Republican Party (PRP) paved the way for the creation of political order in which the Republican Peoples' Party (RPP) held virtually unquestioned rule over the ideological and political administration of the country. Executive leadership over the nascent branches of the government fell to a small coterie of officers and functionaries who, for the most part, had long demonstrated strong personal loyalty to the Gazi. As Mustafa gradually distanced himself from the day-to-day demands of governance, it was these trusted individuals who, again for the most part, served as the main conductors and directors of political affairs in the country. As he had during the closing stages of the War of Independence, Kemal relied heavily upon the assistance and advice of İsmet, who served as state's prime minister during much of the 1920s and 1930s. His relationship with his former lieutenant, however, was often prone to disagreement and brief periods of estrangement, a trend that manifested itself in his relationship with other prominent supporters. In 1930, he called upon his old friend and comrade from Macedonia, Fethi Okyar, to form an opposition party in the hopes of fostering greater debate within the halls of the Grand National Assembly. Fethi's stage-managed efforts to establish the Free Republican Party ultimately met with disaster. Fear of providing provincial voters with a tool to express their outrage toward the government's policies, as well as internal party trepidation toward contesting the will of the president, led to the closure of the party within months of its formation.

Successive terms to the post of president did not temper the pace with which Mustafa Kemal pursued his work and passions. Often rising late, he spent much of his day reading the news and scholarly books. By his death he collected an impressive library of works covering a wide range of topics written in both Turkish and foreign languages. The copious notes and observations he composed longhand within his private library would often be put to use during long dinner conversations held on an almost nightly basis with friends and visitors. Work and pleasure casually over-lapped during these late-night sessions in debates over history and politics. As he had done during the first years in office, Kemal habitually toured Anatolia on official business as well as for per-sonal pleasure. Between visiting farms and schools and making speeches in different corners of the country, he regularly sought the comforts of sailing and bathing at the seashore and in the mineral baths found in the western portion of Turkey. Ironically, Mustafa favored Sultan Abdülhamid II's former Baroque palace, Dolmabahçe, in Istanbul as a place to rest and greet distinguished guests.

Weighty ideas and debates captivated much of Mustafa Kemal's attention during the many discussions, visits, and retreats he un-dertook during his presidency. The establishment of the republic had abolished, in principle, virtually all of the imperial institu-tions that had governed Anatolia during the preceding decades or centuries. While the demolition of the old Ottoman order had ensured Ankara's mandate to rule, the reforms set in motion by the National Movement had left an immense ideological and cul-tural void. In the absence of the sultan/caliph, the *şeyülislam*, the CUP, and various territorial and governmental appendages of the old empire, defining what it meant to be a Turk required an entirely new institutions and ideologues fitting of a self-styled "modern republic". According to Kemal's own reckoning, recon-struction the country's national identity firstly necessitated the exploration and propagation of a new national ethos, one grounded in correcting or erasing the presumed inequities and failures of the Ottoman past. This intellectual and political proj-ect assumed the central focus of his life until his passing at the end of the 1930s.

Articulating the national character of the state he served was a challenge that had naturally occupied Mustafa's interests before assuming the presidency. While his youthful impressions of what it precisely meant to be a Turk in the empire remains fundamentally unclear, the War of Independence, as well as the wartime and postwar cleansing of the country's Christian minorities, appeared to have greatly conditioned how he defined nationality and ethnicity in the republic after 1923. Woodrow Wilson's Fourteen Points had compelled Kemal and others within the National Movement to portray Anatolia in essential ethno-national terms.

His public appeals to the supposed Muslim and Turkish majority of Anatolia did not deter him from asserting more private admonishments toward the clerical authority and apparent religious rigidity found in the country. The sultan/caliph's opposition to Ankara government's authority added greater rancor to Mustafa's anti-clerical opinions (opinions that he first voiced as a young officer). The elimination of the Ottoman royal family, and the religious and imperial offices associated with it, ultimately provided him with more than just the leverage needed to strengthen Ankara's political authority. With the assistance of several critical advisors and subordinates, he incrementally set out to establish a new national ethos that sublimated Islam as a political and social force of influence. Passage of new civil and criminal statutes (including such measures as the hat law) and the establishment of the Ministry of Religious Affairs underscored the desires of the president and his supporters in the RPP to imbue both state and society with a new culture premised upon secular principles. Despite having once presented himself as a defender of Islam and the Islamic world, Mustafa Kemal's writings and statements from his years in office make it clear that he took the predominately Muslim character of the republic's populace for granted. Nevertheless, Islam as a system of practices and beliefs, in his reading of both the past and present, defined neither Turkish citizenship nor identity. In a speech before a crowd in Kastamonu in 1925, he challenged his listeners to not think of the Republic of Turkey as a "land of sheikhs and dervishes." "The truest way, the correct way," he suggested, "is the way of civilization."[2] In defining Turkish civilization, Kemal would ardently maintain that language, history, and race formed the most essential building blocks in the makings of the nation he led and represented.

The Turkish Mustafa Kemal wrote and spoke for most of his life reflected the diversity and richness of the Ottoman Empire's historical evolution. As the written word, Ottoman Turkish was a language that employed an immense vocabulary comprising expressions and grammatical constructs derived from Arabic, Farsi, Greek, Slavic, and Latin, as well as Turkic languages. His spoken Turkish, by all accounts, favored the dialectical traits of Turkish speakers from the capital of Istanbul as well as the southern Balkans. Compared to those native or nonnative speakers coming from other portions of the empire (including Anatolia), Mustafa's diction and accent possessed an air of cosmopolitan breeding and urbanity. Yet he and others influenced by the political ideas of the Committee of Union and Progress (CUP) came to see reform of the Ottoman imperial language as a necessary project for the good of the state. Beginning in the latter years of the Abdülhamid II's reign, young intellectuals began to contemplate a program entailing the simplification of the language in the hopes of combating the high levels of illiteracy in the empire. Nascent national sentiments also guided late Ottoman attempts to reform the Turkish language. Inspired by the works Ziya Gökalp and other figures aligned with the CUP, a growing number of prominent Ottoman intellectuals sought to cleanse Turkish of foreign words and perhaps replace the use of Arabic script with a modified version of the Latin alphabet. Gökalp's ideas, as well as the works of other native and foreign-born intellectuals and scholars, greatly impacted how Mustafa Kemal came to interpret the politics of language education and reform in the republican years. Throughout his presidency, he pored over surveys of grammar, literature, and history, taking particular interest in the linguistic and historical traits of Central Asian Turkic culture. He took great care in noting the supposed similarities or common aspects of Anatolian Turkish and Turkic and Mongol dialects from the Eurasian steppe (in his reading of one study of Turkish grammar, for example, he underlined one passage explaining the Mongol and Manchu root of the Turkish word "to sleep").[3]

His close study of linguistics and history provided the foundation and justification for a series of abrupt and dramatic educational and cultural reforms targeting the Turkish language. In 1928, Ankara mandated the adoption of a revised Latin script (called the Gazi alphabet) and the complete abandonment of Arabic letters and shorthand. The decree appalled many inside and outside of the capital since the Arabic alphabet served not only as the script of the Ottoman language but also the Koran. Kemal dismissed such claims with disdain, stating that Arabic letters comprised "incomprehensible signs that we cannot understand and that squeeze our minds in an iron frame."[4] The president took the lead in proselytizing the new Turkish alphabet, often holding impromptu lectures among small audiences and personally chiding those who resisted the reforms. In 1932, he commissioned the establishment of the Turkish Language Society. He expressly allocated to members of the society the ambitious task of purging the contemporary Turkish lexicon of words deemed foreign or antiquated. In the place of expressions and grammatical structures derived from Ottoman Turkish, the society conceived of a grand series of "pure Turkish" words drawn or devised from Central Asian or classical Turkic sources. The production of this new vulgar Turkish immediately gave way to bizarre and conflicting results. The official abandonment of the Ottoman lexicon forced governmental institutions, as well as private individuals and organizations, to issue books, newspapers, and broadcasts in a language few readily comprehended. The Turkish Language Society's reforms proved so dramatic and unintelligible that dictionaries were required to read the government's modern Turkish. While Kemal embraced these reforms genuinely and rigorously until his death, the bulk of Turkey's citizenry, including individuals closely associated with the Gazi himself, continued to speak and write in the old imperial language and script.

With the passage of generations since his death in 1938, the language reforms of the early republican era did eventually take hold. The high degree of illiteracy found in Turkey at the founding of the republic (which totaled perhaps over 90% of the population) assured the transmission and retention of Mustafa Kemal's modern Turkish. Yet certain costs have accompanied the success of this attempt at rational reform. Virtually no present-day reader of the *Nutuk* is capable of understanding Atatürk's words as he originally intended; instead, a contemporary Turkish speaker requires almost a complete translation of the speech into the modern language. Likewise, almost the entire scope of printed Ottoman and Republican sources (including books and government documents) produced before 1928 remain unintelligible or inaccessible to anyone who has not specifically studied pre-reform Turkish. The impact that Kemalist-era language reform has had upon the historical consciousness of Turks born after 1923 is immense. Without the ability to personally approach and comprehend written documents from the past, an individual raised and educated in modern Turkish fundamentally lacks the tools to assess and commiserate with witnesses to the republic's imperial history. As a consequence, a profound barrier exists between modern Turks and their Ottoman antecedents, creating a contemporary political and social culture that, by design, is largely divorced from Anatolia's immediate and more distant imperial past.

Alienating the republic's citizens from the preceding Ottoman order was clearly among the goals Mustafa Kemal intended to achieve with his sponsorship of Ankara's language reforms. Propagation of a new language, in the president's own estimation, was intimately linked with the crafting of a new history for the peoples of Turkey. The breadth of books found in his personal study testifies to the president's deep interest in historical matters. In addition to works covering the Ottoman Empire, he examined several books and academic pamphlets on Islamic, Central Asia, and European history, archeology, ethnography, and anthropology. He particularly favored recent works and general studies produced in central Europe, which led him to seek out translations and attend lectures by prominent scholars from a variety of fields. By the early 1930s, Kemal had begun to articulate his own interpretations of the genuine history of modern Turks. With the aid of the Turkish Historical Society, an agency first established at Ankara's behest in 1931, he charted out a grand historical outline of the Turkish Republic's past, one that alternately ignored or belittled the state's Ottoman roots.

The Turkish historical thesis, as the Gazi defined it, was anchored in the development of human history in Central Asia. It was upon Eurasia's vast steppe that humanity first took shape. The language spoken by these early peoples was, at its core, a Turkish language. Even after humanity's colonization of the globe's seven continents, all the world's languages retained elements of the language by this proto-Turkish people. Each of the great civilizations, be it ancient Sumaria, Rome, or China, possessed a common Turkish origin. All the great innovations that informed man's passage into modernity were equally the byproduct of Turkish genius and ingenuity.

Strong racial underpinnings further augmented the linguistic aspects of this historical thesis (which was specifically referred to as the "sun theory" of human linguistic development). According to Mustafa Kemal's own reading of the past, modern Turks living in the republic formed a racially superior people akin to the Caucasians of Europe. As the direct inheritors of the Ur-Turkish peoples of Central Asia, they embodied the prime physiological, intellectual, and aesthetic ideals of the white Caucasian race. The Gazi utilized a number of venues to advocate for the Turkish historical thesis. In addition to opening the Turkish Historical Society (which became the primary vehicle for Kemal's historical principles), the RPP co-opted the work of the Turkish Hearths organization, an educational and cultural organization established during the late CUP period. The Turkish Hearths came to champion the government's interpretation of the past, with members teaching regular, and often officially compulsory, lessons on language and history in hundreds of "Peoples' Houses" opened throughout the country. Mustafa took an active role in crafting an elementary history textbook, entitled *The Outlines of Turkish History*, as well as *Civic Knowledge*, a schoolbook on Turkey's unique political and civic values. Even the exercise of religious rites did not fall beyond the purview of Ankara's effort toward Turkification. Beginning in 1928, homilies delivered before congregations assembled for Friday prayers were performed in Turkish. Atatürk's dictum that "henceforth the Turkish language predominate every level of religion" was eventually extended to the call to prayer and the reading of the Koran, which had been annunciated, since the time of the Prophet Mohammed, in the Arabic language.[5]

THE NATION'S MENTOR. *The Gazi tests and demonstrates the use of a new tractor in 1929.*

The Turkish historical thesis clashed with innumerable fundamental political, social, and cultural realities that defined the young republic. In addition to suggesting that all the peoples of the world were, to some extent, Turks, the sun theory implied that each of the country's citizens spoke Turkish. How could a citizen not speak Turkish since it was counted as, in his own summation, "one of the most beautiful, richest and easiest" languages one could learn in the world?[6] Yet many of the people living in Turkey during Mustafa Kemal's reign certifiably did not speak Turkish (let alone master the modern Turkish Ankara promoted). While World War I and the War of Independence may have resulted in the expulsion and killing of most of Anatolia's Christian population, the early Turkish Republic continued to be inhabited by an immense array of indigenous and immigrant Muslim groups. Turkey's diverse Muslim population in the 1920s and 1930s comprised unknown thousands of native and recently settled Arabs, Bosnians, Kurds, Albanians, Circassians, and Turks (which, as a polity, was subdivided into dialectical and, in certain areas, tribal factions). Claims regarding the inherent racial superiority of Turks posed unsettling prospects for the country's Jewish communities, who, according to the dogmas of European proponents of racial theory, were a degenerative group set apart from the otherwise pure Caucasian majority. The proposition that all of the classical cultures of the world were, at heart, Turkish in origin lastly defied the global consensus regarding the many layers of history that informed the republic's pre-imperial past. Virtually no contemporary archeologist would consent to the notion that ancient Assyrian, Hittite, Greek, or Roman historical sites were the product of Turkish ingenuity. All in all, few beyond Mustafa Kemal's circle of supporters in Ankara believed in, let alone intuitively abided by, the president's spacious and radical rendition of Turkey's culture and past.

In 1931, Recep Peker, a high-ranking RPP official who was of North Caucasian descent, made the following observations:

We consider as ourselves all those of our citizens who live among us, who belong politically and socially to the Turkish Nation and among whom ideas and feelings such as "Kurdism," "Circassianism," and even "Lazism" and "Pomakism" have been implanted. We deem it our duty to banish, by sincere efforts, those false conceptions, which are a legacy of an absolutist regime and the product of long-standing historical oppression. The scientific truth of today does not allow an independent existence of a nation of several hundred thousand, or even of a million individuals. . . . We want to state just as sincerely our opinion regarding our Jewish or Christian compatriots. Our party considers these compatriots as absolutely Turkish insofar as they belong to our community of language and ideal.[7]

Recep's words almost completely mirror words uttered previously by Mustafa Kemal, who similarly stated that "the individuals of this nation [who claim to be Kurds, Circassians, Bosnians, or Laz], like the whole Turkish community, are in possession of a common past, history, morality and law."[8] Beginning in the late 1920s, lawmakers and bureaucrats in Ankara set out to render the implications of the Turkish historical thesis a resolute political and social reality. The Grand National Assembly passed multiple measures encouraging or forcing natives and immigrants alike to speak Turkish both at home and in public. Provincial government officials contributed to this new façade by changing the names of scores of Greek, Armenian, Kurdish, and Arabic-speaking villages and towns in favor of new Turkish names. In the wake of the 1923 population exchange with Greece, potential immigrants arriving to the republic were forced to contend with new laws meant to screen and exclude subversive non-Turkish peoples. Arabs, Roma, and Albanians were expressly banned from entering the country while other migrants from the Balkans and the Caucasus were compelled to demonstrate intrinsically Turkish qualities. Despite having denied any responsibility or guilt in carrying out the deportation and murder of non-Muslims during the course of the war years, Ankara categorically rejected attempts by Armenians, Greeks, and Syriac Christians to return to Anatolia. The RPP also maintained the old CUP practice of resettling native and immigrant Muslim populations throughout the country, a policy that resulted in the uprooting and internal deportation of thousands of communities.

Ankara's efforts toward diluting or limiting the influence of potentially subversive non-Turkish groups and communities attained more capricious dimensions with the passage of the so-called Surname Law in 1934. Throughout the history of the Ottoman Empire and the early republic, most Muslims bore no family name that would be passed down from one generation to the next. Men and women instead referred to one another with reference to either the names of the fathers ("son or daughter of Ahmet"), their point of origin (*Selanikli* Mustafa or Mustafa from Selanik), a distinctive physical feature (Kara Hasan or Hasan with black hair), or ethno-linguistic traits (Arab Abdullah or Abdullah the Arab). Even more common expressions of self-identification came in the form of military, religious, or formal titles (such as Pasha, *hoca*, or *efendi*). In the late 1920s, the Grand National Assembly began to reverse this trend by forbidding Turkish citizens from referring to themselves or others with specific non-Turkish ethnic epithets (thus making any reference to one's Albanian, Arab, Circassian, or Kurdish ethnic heritage illegal). In 1934, Ankara went further still and revoked the use of any formal military or religious titles or ranks. In the place of these markers of status or ethnicity, the government mandated that all Turkish citizens adopt a contrived Turkish surname of their choosing. Local administrators compelled or encouraged citizens to adopt strong or masculine names during the registration process, leading many to adopt such patronyms as Özdemir (True Iron), Korkmaz (Fearless), or Yıldırım (Thunder). At times, the awarding of new names took on arbitrary characteristics. For example, when one man working in his fields failed to appear to register, agents declared, "This is a very *geniş* man, a very relaxed man. Let his surname be Geniş."[9] In November 1934, Mustafa Kemal chose for himself a name fitting his role and stature within the young republic. In taking the name Atatürk, "father of the Turks," he chose to dispense with the use of Mustafa, the name bestowed to him by his mother. He henceforth signed all documents Kemal Atatürk, erroneously arguing that the name he received in his early school years was not of Arabic but of Turkish origin.

Popular reaction to Ankara's generalized policy of Turkification can be described as mixed at best. Many local peoples continued to use honorific and ethnic nicknames and titles when referring to their neighbors and social betters. Many Turks, into their old age, would rarely, if ever, adopt their surnames in everyday parlance (to the point of forgetting the names they had chosen for themselves). The spread of a rigid educational curriculum that emphasized the country's mythic Turkish past and culture had only a moderate impact upon communities that spoke Kurdish, Arabic, or other languages. Despite the government's best efforts to prevent non-Turks from entering and establishing new lives in Anatolia (a trend that had begun well before 1923), ethnic Bosnians, Chechens, Iranians, Albanians, and Arabs did manage to pass across Turkey's borders and settle among native and immigrant communities alike. From his lofty perch in the president's mansion in Ankara, it is unclear to what degree Kemal perceived or comprehended these everyday forms of opposition.

Resistance to the government's nationalizing regime did become confrontational at various points of Atatürk's reign. In 1933, Muslims praying at the central mosque in Bursa held protests against the abrogation of Arabic as the language of Islamic worship. The leaders of the demonstration were promptly arrested. Three years earlier, in the Aegean town of Menemen, a local holy man (or dervish) gathered together a crowd of believers and declared himself the messiah sent by God to punish the Turkish government for its transgressions against Islam. When a contingent of troops attempted to intervene and quell the demonstration, the unit's commander was shot and beheaded. The Menemen incident elicited a cold and uncompromising reaction from Mustafa Kemal, who demanded the town be razed to the ground for having defied Ankara's authority. A bloody reprisal against the rebels and the townspeople was averted after İsmet, then serving as prime minister, promised to investigate the incident and punish those responsible.

Perhaps the most violent display of antagonism toward Ankara's policy was manifested among the country's Kurdish population. In 1930, a Kurdish nationalist organization based in Beirut, called Khoybun, organized a revolt in the mountainous region enveloping Mount Ararat, located close to Turkey's frontier with Iran and Soviet Armenia. Leaders of the Ararat insurrection, unlike Sheikh Said, rose in rebellion with the explicit hopes of establishing an independent Kurdish state, a state that had been denied to Turkey's Kurds with the signing of the Treaty of Lausanne. Ankara's response to Khoybun's demands was initially conciliatory in the hopes of negotiating a peaceful return to order in this area along the border. When Kurdish insurgents rejected the government's diplomatic overtures, two corps of army regulars were deployed to Ararat. Suppression of the Khoybun uprising lasted months as rebels staged dramatic attacks both along the frontier as well as to the west and south in Diyabakir, Mardin, and Urfa. When the fighting finally ebbed to a standstill, Ankara instituted a new regime of martial law throughout eastern Anatolia "in the interest of public order."[10]

The imposition of military rule, as well as concomitant acts of deportation and armed suppression, did not forestall the outbreak of a second rebellion in the region of Dersim in 1937. As a province that had risen in revolt during the course of the War of Independence, tensions remained high between local Kurdish Shiites and appointed officials throughout the early republican era. Relations between the government and the indigenous population exploded after the passage of multiple laws demanding further integration of the region into the new norms of the Turkish government (laws that included renaming the region Tunceli, meaning "iron fist" in Turkish). When a delegation of notables seeking an audience with the local military governor was placed under arrest in January 1937, protestors ambushed policemen, cut telegraph wires, and burned bridges. The Turkish military, unlike in the case of the Ararat rebellion, wasted little time in initiating armed operations against the Kurdish insurgents. Over the course of a year's time, army units established a strict cordon around Dersim, restricting both local and outsiders (including journalists) from entering or leaving the mountainous region. The full might of the Turkish armed forces was brought to bear in suppressing the rebels, an effort that included the use of warplanes and "burning and asphyxiating" chemical bombs.[11] Tens of thousands of people were killed or deported once armed hostilities came to a close in 1938. Mustafa Kemal's adopted daughter, Sabiha Gökçen, personally partook in military operations against Dersim's Kurds as a bomber pilot. While the participation of a woman (the president's daughter no less) may have constituted a breakthrough in women's rights, Atatürk did voice some apprehension toward Sabiha's service. After stating that he would be heartbroken if she was shot down and taken prisoner, Kemal's daughter assured him that "the Kurds would not take me." "At the time I jump from my plane I will commit suicide," she promised, "I have a revolver at my side."[12]

The earnestness with which officials in Ankara subdued Kurds and religious conservatives was equally applied toward the economy. Mustafa Kemal and his supporters in the capital contended with an Anatolian economy long beset by dysfunction and structural weaknesses. The sheer devastation of World War I and the War of Independence only compounded these historic limitations. As a result of these wars, the young republican government was forced to confront immediately urgent problems such as resettling refugees and reconstructing scores of devastated towns and villages, as well as addressing Turkey's endemically poor and underdeveloped transport system, inefficient agricultural sector, limited industrial base, and weak banks. Ankara's generalized program of Turkification was immediately applied in attempting to solve these manifold challenges. Land and property belonging to non-Muslim residents who had been displaced or dispatched by the fighting or Ankara's population agreement with Greece became an important means of addressing the problems of unemployment, landlessness, and reconstruction. Atatürk, beginning with his first days in office in 1920, became an outspoken champion of modernization of Turkey's agricultural industry. He was a frequent visitor and speaker at newly opened technical schools, congresses, and model farms (especially within the vicinity of Ankara). In keeping with his roots as a Young Turk, he did not abandon the wartime administration's intent to build a culture of Muslim entrepreneurialism and the establishment of an economy free of direct foreign influence. The realities of the postwar era, particularly after the onset of the Great Depression, forced the president to reconsider these principles to some degree. France, for example, retained some economic rights it had enjoyed as a result of the settlements following World War I. Foreign migrants, particularly those escaping the rise of National Socialism in Central Europe, played important roles in building Turkey's budding educational system. More important, the lack of private capital and knowhow compelled Ankara to take invasive steps into the nation's economy. Toward the end of the 1930s, a variety of state bureaucratic offices assumed ownership and responsibility for numerous sectors of economic activity. A new system of official agricultural and industrial monopolies came into existence while state officials undertook the arduous task of building roads and expanding the nation's skeletal railway system. As Kemal put it in a statement to the nation in 1935, the state would take the task of "realizing our industrialization programs, the issuing and protection of the excellence and standards of our products, the expansion of every form of the sea economy, the growth of all aspects of the metals economy, and the standardization of our small credit organizations."[13] As ambitious as these goals were, and as active as Mustafa was in proselytizing new methods and standards, Turkey experienced little economic growth by the time of the president's death.

The Republican Peoples' Party proved somewhat more successful in other attempts at imprinting the Gazi's will and ideals upon the government. The dismantling of old Ottoman offices and the establishment of new bureaus in Ankara continued apace after the closure of the caliphate. One institution handled with special care during this period of transition was the nation's military. The army that had acculturated Mustafa Kemal into politics changed during the course of the first years of the republic. Under the tenure of the army's chief of staff, Fevzi Çakmak, the Turkish military ceased to be a hotbed of intrigue and factionalism. While most of the most high-ranking and well-respected generals escaped imprisonment or execution in the aftermath of the Izmir plot, the RPP administration was successful in limiting the political influence of prominent officers and the army as a whole. Nevertheless, Ankara did not disregard the military's service during the War of Independence in incorporating it under the guise of the country's new national ethos. Like the Ottoman army before, Turkey's armed service was cast as the vanguard of the nation, guiding it through its travails and assuring it of greater fortunes ahead. The military's activities, as the Gazi articulated in his treatise on Turkish civics, did not simply entail fighting at the front; "securing the inviolability of [the state's] independence" was a goal that enjoined the army alongside the rest of the civilian population.[14] In a speech before a military club in 1931, Atatürk was laudatory and expansive in delineating the role he foresaw for Turkey's army:

> You know that whenever the Turkish nation has wanted to stride towards the heights it has always seen its army, which is composed of its own heroic sons, as the permanent leader in the forefront of this march, as a the permanent vanguard in campaigns to bring

lofty ideals to reality. . . . In times to come, also, its heroic soldier sons will march in the vanguard for the attainment of the sublime ideals of the Turkish nation.[15]

A law passed in 1935 helped to actualize the president's vision of the military as a matter of official policy. Rather than simply embodying the spirit and principles of the republic, the law stipulated that the military possessed a legal obligation to defend both the state and its constitution. The implication of the statute, as officers would later interpret it, seemed to suggest that the army had a role to play in managing (to the point of circumscribing) the civilian government's behavior when either the state or its constitution was under threat.

In 1937, the RPP, under the president and chairman's direction, finally distilled and crystallized the core principles of the Gazi's worldview. While never claiming that Atatürk's political vision formed a coherent ideology, the RPP's executive body maintained that six core principles served as the essential planks that buttressed the state. The Six Arrows, as they were called, comprised dense and sweeping values that Turkey's founder had repeatedly appealed to and cited since 1923: republicanism, populism, nationalism, secularism, etatism, and revolutionism. With his death in 1938, the Six Arrows ceased to be identified solely with the RPP. Instead, each element of this political program came to be further embellished and memorialized as fundamental to Kemalism, an ideology that since has informed the thoughts and actions of generations of Turkish politicians, military officers, and common citizens.

Foreign policy was not immune to the emerging dogmas of Kemalism. In a 1931 address, Atatürk described the cornerstone of his government's approach toward international relations in one simple aphorism: "We are working for peace at home and peace in the world."[16] In hindsight, this uncomplicated perspective upon world affairs underscored a basic pragmatism toward issues of regional security and cooperation. In the aftermath of the Treaty of Lausanne, Kemal abandoned most of the unfulfilled territorial claims made under the aegis of the Grand National Assembly's National Pact. Western Thrace, with its large Muslim population, was abandoned to Greece. Even the old Ottoman province of Mosul, which İsmet had staunchly maintained at Lausanne was an integral Turkish territory, was ceded without prejudice to Iraq after the League of Nations ruled in Baghdad's favor. The sole stretch of land that remained a point of contention was the region enveloping the town of Iskenderun, which the French mandate of Syria had acquired as a result of the Treaty of Sèvres. Ankara's disengagement from territorial questions shifted markedly during the mid-1930s when political upheaval in Syria opened the possibility of a change in the mandate's borders. Per the stipulations of the Sèvres Treaty, Iskenderun's Turkish-speaking population was guaranteed the right of cultural autonomy, a status that led to the localized adaptation of several reforms undertaken to the north in Turkey (reforms which included similar laws on the wearing of hats and the use of a Latin alphabet). Moreover, nationalists in both the republic and in Iskenderun placated the region's mythic Turkish past, with both sides claiming that the region was historically bound to Anatolia since the ancient Hittite peoples, a proto-Turkish group in their estimation, had long inhabited both sides of the border. When Paris granted Syria independence in 1936, nationalists in Hatay (as Turkish nationalists called the province) demanded the right to secede with an eye toward unification with the Turkish Republic. Intervention by the League of Nations, as well as France's unwillingness to antagonize Turkey, ultimately led to a rigged local election that certified Turkish nationalist demands. Mustafa Kemal, who had supported the inclusion of this dubiously ancient Turkish territory into the republic, did not live to see Hatay's union with Turkey in 1939. Nevertheless, when the topic was broached with him before his death, he explicitly pointed to Nazi Germany's acquisition of Austria in March 1938. "Hitler is absolutely correct," he declared, "Germans belong with Germans."[17]

Aside from Ankara's aggressive stance toward Syria, Mustafa Kemal personally oversaw the development of a Turkish foreign policy that accentuated the need to form strong bilateral and multilateral relations with the country's immediate neighbors and former rivals. Beginning with the Treaty of Lausanne, the new Turkish foreign ministry, headed by long-time diplomat Rüştü Aras, launched a series of initiatives leading to numerous agreements stipulating mutual relations based upon peace, non-aggression, and cooperation. In addition to establishing a Treaty of Friendship with Greece in 1930, Ankara signed an agreement of neutrality with Italy, a state that had previously invaded Anatolia and was threatening military expansion into the Mediterranean. When Rome continued to press its expansionist agenda within Turkey's immediate vicinity, Ankara moved to establish stronger ties with the Balkan states of Greece, Romania, and Yugoslavia in the hopes of assuring a state of peace among neighbors as well as mutual recognition of each other's borders. A similar agreement of mutual recognition and cooperation was signed three years later in Sadabad with the eastern states of Iraq, Iran, and Afghanistan.

The Balkan agreements forged by Aras and Atatürk also serviced another important aspect of the country's foreign and domestic policy. The end of the Balkan Wars and the abolition of the Ottoman Empire did not completely put to rest questions about the status of hundreds of thousands of Muslims living within the fledgling states of Albania, Yugoslavia, Bulgaria, and Romania. In Yugoslavia and Bulgaria, in particular, native Muslims experienced successive waves of violence at the hands of the central government in the aftermath of World War I. Facing the prospect of further acts of violence (which, like in Turkey, often came in the name of nationalizing the country's diverse population), many Muslims had sought to flee to Anatolia in the hopes of a better life. Authorities in Ankara were aware of the plight of many of the Ottoman Empire's former Muslim citizens and, throughout the 1920s and 1930s, sought to influence and manage this steady flow of refugees. Beginning with Armenia in 1920, the Turkish Foreign Ministry sealed several agreements with neighboring states facilitating the mass transfer of Muslims into Turkey. While these newcomers were subject to the country's rigorous scrutiny (since acceptance of asylum was premised upon an individual demonstrating supposed racial and ethnic attributes of a Turk), Mustafa and his close advisors valued the introduction of Muslim refugees into Turkish society as a means of further Turkifying regions of Anatolia inhabited by Kurds. He personally partook in negotiations on the question of immigration with representatives from the Kingdom of Yugoslavia, a state that was attempting to forcibly deport virtually all of its Muslim citizens from the regions of Kosova and Macedonia.

The threat of a second generalized war between the great powers of Europe did provide Kemal with some cause for concern as the 1930s progressed. Italy's unprovoked invasion of Albania and Ethiopia, as well as the steady remilitarization of Germany's frontier, called into question Turkey's immediate security. While attempting to revitalize the nation's stock of armaments, the president's foreign representatives attempted to secure better relations with each of Europe's potential combatants. As in the case of Greece, Atatürk was vocal in eschewing Turkey's previous grievances with both Great Britain and France and took deliberate personal steps in engaging British and French diplomats on issues of war and peace. His administration sought equally warm relations with Germany and the Soviet Union, despite some domestic fears that Moscow would attempt to exact territorial demands upon Turkey in the case of war. Mustafa Kemal's policy of neutrality within the context of Europe was best exemplified during the convening of talks in 1936 on the military status of the Bosphorus and Dardanelles Straits. According to the Montreaux agreement of that year, Turkey was afforded the right to ban all military vessels in times of war (regardless of whether Ankara remained a neutral party or not). Thus, with the same stroke of the pen, Turkish diplomats achieved both the right to retain total sovereign control over the straits as well as assert greater leverage as a neutral party in the event of conflict within the eastern Mediterranean.

Regardless of the diplomatic questions confronting his government, Mustafa Kemal made it a personal matter to meet with foreign leaders and their representatives. He took great pleasure in dining and carousing during state visits and frequently offered tours of the coastline upon the president's yacht (an experience enjoyed, for example, by British monarch Edward VIII). In entertaining foreign guests, he consciously endeavored to present himself and his country as paragons of positive and progressive reformation. The president frequently engaged his guests in heady conversations on politics, culture, and history in the midst of dinner parties, military parades, visits to state schools, and other events. In addition to showing off the country's material and historical wealth (as seen in many of Turkey's newly established archeological museums), the Gazi also entreated guests to visit the ground where he had earned fame as a military commander outside of Gallipoli. His conscious efforts to present Turkey's modernity in the best possible light caused some moments of official discomfort, such as during the official visit of Iran's emperor, Reza Shah. As the two statesmen pulled into a station outside of the western town of Uşak in 1934, Kemal viewed a man wearing a turban standing among a crowd of well-wishers. Upon seeing this outward display of religiosity (which was in defiance of the country's hat law), the president charged the gathering of cheering citizens to "destroy him" since clerics were "the enemy of the people." While the man in the turban purportedly escaped with his life, Atatürk subsequently banned the display of religious garb outside of mosques.[18]

While never venturing abroad as president, the Gazi's concerted effort toward public diplomacy, both inside and outside of Turkey, did earn his young nation the kind of international status he had longed to cultivate since his days as an officer. Turkey was no longer seen as an entity analogous to the Ottoman Empire, a state

A NEW POLITICAL LANDSCAPE. *Citizens file past a statue of Atatürk astride a horse in the midst of Ankara.*

that had been historically maligned by European states as a weak, reactionary, and impotent hulk residing at the crossroads between East and West. In choosing to finally join the League of Nations in 1932, Turkey assumed the standing of other influential states in Europe and Asia. While Ankara failed to retain a lasting seat in the League's main council, there was little "doubt of the psychological value" of being a member of the body, as one contemporary American observer put it.[19] Ankara had surpassed their imperial predecessors in establishing Turkey as constructive members of the contemporary global order.

Joining the Western modern world, in Mustafa Kemal's eyes, entailed more than achieving a place at the same table as the European powers. Nationalizing the politics, economy, and culture of the country, making it unquestionably Turkish, reflected the president's deepest desires to shape state and society in a way that conformed to Western norms. The effort to raise Turkish civilization to the highest of standards went beyond addressing questions of borders, agricultural policy, or religious or linguistic discourse. Throughout his reign, Atatürk expressed pointed interest in modernizing and nationalizing basic social interactions. He was an earnest promoter of theater, music, and art. His taste in culture represented, in hindsight, some conflicting aspects of his political vision. On the one hand, the RPP encouraged the development and spread of popular culture that celebrated ethnic Turkish traditions. While Ankara recognized and endorsed a new national dance (based upon the folk dances of the Turkish-speaking Zeybek peoples of western Anatolia), Turkey's fledgling radio stations attempted to popularize native ballads and rural folk music (*türkü*) among its listeners. On the other hand, the Gazi made no secret of his affection for jazz and modern art. He made numerous public appearances at parties and cafes where jazz music was played and at times delighted in dancing the foxtrot. His regime embraced modernist tendencies in painting and sculpture, particularly in works that celebrated the wartime victories and feats he achieved alongside his loyal lieutenants.

Reshaping the status of women in the new republic was an integral part of how Kemal distilled and attended to the development of modern culture in Turkey. In 1925, before a meeting of the RPP, he addressed the status of women in this regard:

> In many places I see women who have a kerchief or towel thrown over their head, with their face and eyes hidden, who turn away to men who pass by or sit down with their eyes closed. What is the sense and meaning of this behavior? Gentlemen, should the mothers and daughters of a civilized nation go on behaving in such a barbaric manner? That is a sight which portrays the nation in an extremely ridiculous way. One must immediately correct this.[20]

These outward displays of feminine behavior were symptomatic, in Atatürk's estimation, of two trends that required redress. Mirroring opinions he voiced to fellow officers during World War I, he used his offices to promote greater political, personal, and labor rights for women. In addition to extending the vote to women in 1930, Ankara created a national labor union for women, an organization that advocated on the behalf of the growing number of female students, workers, and professionals active in the Turkish economy. The increasing degree to which the Kemalist state sought to address women's political and social standing paralleled complementary public and private initiatives designed to make women physically and socially more visible as actors in the republic. The wearing of headscarves, which was not banned outright, would become prohibited within the confines of public buildings. A growing body of magazines and books celebrating and detailing the lives of women came into being. The enhanced personal freedoms the RPP endowed to women particularly came into national and international focus when Keriman Halis, a Turkish citizen of Albanian descent, won the Miss Universe competition in 1932. This achievement, like so many other changes taking place in Turkey, was popularly attributed to the personal intervention of Mustafa Kemal himself. Upon her victory, Keriman telegrammed the president, declaring that her success was "the result of the ideas inspired by you in the women of our country."[21]

By his later years, the Gazi's advocacy on women's issues resonated strongly within the confines of his personal life. His divorce from Latife left a void never to be filled by another spouse. Although fond of flirting and dancing with women in his company, he remained a bachelor to his death. The ranks of his family grew instead through his adoption of several children beginning in 1924. While he had briefly taken custody of a young boy during World War I (who was ultimately raised in his mother's home), the first child he adopted was Sabiha, who was a twelve-year-old orphan living in Bursa when the president first met her. Sabiha's inclusion into Kemal's household occurred at roughly the same time he adopted four other girls in their teens: Zehra, Rukiye, Afet, and Nebile. A fifth adopted daughter, Ülkü, joined the president's family as a toddler, just three years before his death. Mustafa was forthright in sending each of his adopted daughters to the best schools available to them. Yet by all accounts the relationship between the girls and their father varied dramatically. While young Ülkü was a constant presence at her father's side, Zehra and Rukiye appeared to have had a more distant relationship with Kemal. Of all the young women, Afet enjoyed an exceptionally close attachment with him. As she grew into adulthood, she assumed the role of Atatürk's best student and most intimate stenographer. It was with Afet's assistance that his manual on Turkish civics, *Civic Knowledge*, and his treatise on Turkish history, *The Outlines of Turkish History*, were completed. Shortly before his death, she was accepted into a doctoral program in Geneva where she eventually completed a thesis on the anthropological features of the "Turkish race." She also served as one of her father's closest attendants and confidants, collecting and transcribing numerous recollections and stories from his life. He evidently took special pleasure in remaining in her company. "We were all pleased that Atatürk had found a friend [in Afet] to dispel his sadness," one

THE PRESIDENT'S DAUGHTER. *An entourage of officers and officials accompanies an aging Atatürk and his youngest daughter, Ülkü.*

observer later remarked, "as we were afraid that his nerves would give way."[22]

The sadness attested by this observer no doubt was in part a reference to the ill state of the Gazi's health in the last years of his life. As he entered his fifties, Kemal's dependency upon alcohol was beginning to get the better of him. While he had openly flaunted decorum on more than one occasion in toasting guests and events with a glass of spirits in his hand, there were times when alcohol left the president worse for wear. Diplomatic circles were often rife with gossip of the Kemal's frequent drunkenness, with one ambassador reporting home that the president often drank rakı (a common anise liquor) "all day and occasionally proceeding to a state of complete intoxication by nightfall."[23] During one notorious event in commemoration of the republic's founding in 1926, a series of disquieted partygoers witnessed the president, after having much to drink, attempting to kiss the daughter of the French ambassador, an act that led the diplomat to flee the gathering with his daughter without a word. Mustafa Kemal's alcoholism appears to have been largely interpreted as symptomatic of a life lived intensely. Many agreed that the president was a man who burned "the candle pretty heavily on both ends." Yet early on in his presidency, some could tell that his excessive use of alcohol, as well as his restless lifestyle, was beginning to visibly sap his physical and mental strength.[24]

By 1936, Mustafa developed the first symptoms of an aggravated case of cirrhosis of the liver. When doctors eventually concluded that a series of rashes on the president's body were signs of the disease, he remained in office and continued, to the best of his ability, to remain actively engaged with his duties. Between February and July 1938, he stubbornly attended diplomatic meetings and military reviews, and kept up with the workings of his government. In the summer, he removed himself to the city of Istanbul and took up residence at Dolmabahçe, Abdülhamid II's gilded palace. In July, he fell into a coma that lasted until the end of October. Throughout the intervening months, several of Kemal's closest political advisors attended to his bedside alongside three of his daughters: Afet, Sabiha, and Makbule. He emerged from his coma and remained alert for almost three weeks, during which time he celebrated the country's fifteenth anniversary from his sickbed. On November 8, he slipped back into a coma and died two days later. Among those present at Dolmabahçe that morning was his childhood friend Salih Bozok. Upon seeing his lifeless body, Salih fled from the room and shot himself in the chest. Salih later confessed to his son that he could not remember his actions after he fled from the Gazi's room, even though he insisted that he "could never forget" the day Atatürk died.[25]

The public's reaction to the Gazi's death was swift and sorrowful. When news of his passing first filtered across Istanbul, "all work ceased," the American ambassador reported, "stores and shops were voluntarily closed and crowds of dejected people, many weeping openly, appeared on the streets where for hours they walked aimlessly up and down."[26] Mustafa Kemal's body remained in Dolmabahçe in the days following his death. Public officials ultimately opened the doors of the palace to the public on December 12, allowing thousands of mourners to file past his body as he lay in state. Eight days later a train bore his corpse to the capital for the official funeral. His body was initially interred at Ankara's Ethnographical Museum, one of the capital's first cultural landmarks built during the early republican era. It would take almost fifteen years for Turkish officials to render his casket to its final resting place. In November 1953, builders completed Atatürk's mausoleum. Dubbed Anıtkabir (large memorial), the tomb is an immense complex constructed of concrete, steel, and marble. Housed within are artifacts from his life as well as a museum depicting his struggle to become father of the Turkish nation. Sitting on a hill that was formerly the site of an ancient Greek settlement, Anıtkabir continues to tower over Ankara's skyline.

Seventeen countries sent representatives to bear witness to Kemal's burial. An even larger contingent of newspapers and public figures issued testaments commemorating the life and work of Turkey's first president. One German paper, in citing his victories on the battlefield, and the many reforms passed under the Gazi's watch, heralded him as a man possessing a "will of granite and an inexhaustible work ethic."[27] Even the editors of *The New York Times*, who had decried his struggle for independence as among the worst causes in the world, published a laudatory and deferential epitaph upon news of his death:

> As a soldier and statesmen Kemal Ataturk ranks high in the history of his country. He was without doubt one of the ablest national leaders of the post-war period. The one dictator who let his works speak for him, he was also the only one who actually created the state he ruled. After the Sick Man of Europe had been amputated to the bone, he took the remnants of the Ottoman Empire and shaped them into a modern state, self-reliant and respected. As a result of his rule the diminished Turkey of today is not only a healthier but a far stronger and more stable nation than the vast suzerainty of the Sultans.[28]

Many of those who knew the Gazi personally echoed this judgment rendered upon his life and works. His biographer Şevket Sürreya Aydemir, who knew him while he worked as a writer for a state-run journal, later reflected that most men who die so young often do so with much rancor. The president, a man who "gave meaning to life," did not pass with rancor. Yet for those around him, his loss was akin to the roots of a great tree being pulled from the soil.[29]

CHAPTER 6

| ATATÜRK AS A HISTORICAL |
FIGURE

IN AN ANECDOTE PROVIDED BY Ernest Jäckh, a German scholar who had lived and worked in both the Turkish Republic and the Ottoman Empire, Mustafa Kemal purportedly presumed that his spirit would live on past his death:

> There are two Mustafa Kemals. One is sitting before you, the Mustafa Kemal of flesh and blood, who will pass away. There is another whom I cannot call Me. It is not I that this Mustafa Kemal personifies, it is You—all you present here, who go into the far-thermost parts of the country to inculcate and defend a new ideal, a new mode of thought. I stand for these dreams of yours. My life's work is to make them come true.[1]

The Republican Peoples' Party (RPP) helped to realize this vision soon after his burial. In December 1938, the newly appointed president İsmet İnönü called together the RPP's chief delegates to a meeting and declared, by popular vote, that Atatürk would remain the "eternal leader" of the party. The RPP's decision that December to instate the president as the undying guide and figurehead encapsulated an emerging official culture of worship and devotion that had developed around his person since the first days of the republic. Within two years of the republic's establishment, Mustafa Kemal had already commissioned an Austrian artist to erect the first statue bearing his likeness in Istanbul. By 1938, public officials unveiled a great many more busts and statues of the Gazi in cities and towns throughout the country. While İnönü attempted to fashion a similar status for himself during his presidency (going so far as to assume the title of National Leader during the course of World War II), Kemal's image, as well as his immense corpus of writings and sayings, remained deeply imbedded within the fabric of Turkish education, politics, and culture.

When İsmet and the RPP relinquished its monopoly on power in 1950, the newly elected government of Prime Minister Adnan Menderes embraced Kemal's cult that much further. After a group of dissident Islamists carried out a series of brazen attacks upon monuments to the president in the first years of his rule, Menderes and his governing Democratic Party made it illegal to insult his memory (a crime that still carries with it a penalty of up to three years in prison). The worship and commemoration of Atatürk's life, works, and ideas grew still stronger in the turbulent years following Turkey's first military coup in 1960. Political leaders and voters from across the country's political spectrum continue to pay homage to his memory, often justifying conflicting positions on questions of religion, gender, ethnicity, and the economy on the supposed basis of the Gazi's initial wishes and ideals. Regardless of the degree to which contemporary Islamists, secular leftists, and nationalists of various stripes embrace his legacy, Mustafa Kemal's image (as well as his most noted dictums and his personal signature) adorns the walls of countless offices, classrooms, cafes, and private homes throughout the country. He is still regarded, in many respects, as Turkey's eternal leader and talisman.

Ankara's victory in the War of Independence, as well as the establishment of the republic in 1923, undoubtedly conferred great fame upon the Gazi. One may argue, counterfactually, that his central role in both of these events would have secured for him the status of Turkey's premiere national hero regardless of his actions after 1923. Yet it is because of his tenure as president, particularly after 1926, that he is so universally recognized in momentous and mythic terms. Both then and now, what he achieved following the war seems nothing short of miraculous and, to some degree, unprecedented. He personally provided much of the intellectual framework that led many inside and outside of the country to view Turkey as a state reborn. His leadership, beginning with his own conduct, was instrumental in shaping a new political, social, and economic culture that restored the esteem of the republic's citizens. This new culture, which was explicitly modeled upon modern norms, commanded the respect of a variety of observers abroad (including those residing in countries previously at odds with Ankara). To this day, Atatürk's admirers insist that his reforms made Turks into the people they had long aspired to become: a singular civilized *volk* united around the principles of secularism, ethno-nationalism, and devotion to the state.

However, there were some individuals who lived during the Kemalist era who saw Turkey's founding president in less than stellar terms. Kazim Karabekir, who had served the Nationalist cause faithfully during the War of Independence, levied several criticisms against the Gazi while penning his autobiography. He voiced particular dissent toward the ways in which he wielded power dictatorially, a charge made by others who were politically marginalized after the Izmir trials. The tenor of criticism since 1938 has grown in other quarters inside and outside of Turkey. For many, it is hard to ignore the harshness and brutality with which he and his government suppressed Kurds, Armenians, and devoted Muslims. To this day, in part as a result of the laws forbidding citizens from insulting Mustafa Kemal's memory, public discussion and debate on the merits, flaws, and failures of the RPP's policies during the interwar period remain limited. Publication of Karabekir's memoirs, for example, was forbidden for decades after its first printing. It is only recently that the Turkish government has attempted to come to terms with the violent campaign against Dersim's Kurds in 1937. In an attack upon his rivals in the RPP, Prime Minister Tayyip Erdoğan called upon RPP officials in 2011 to own up to the Dersim massacres, calling it "the most tragic event in recent history."[2]

The extent to which Atatürk is venerated and demonized does beg the question of how one should interpret his policies and legacies as president. Yet rather than opine as to whether he was a visionary or monster, it is perhaps best to view his actions and accomplishments from this era through the lens of his immediate past as well as through the global political context of the interwar period. When one considers his political upbringing as a Young Turk, as well as the approaches of other authoritarian leaders from the immediate postwar years, the Gazi's many accomplishments and excesses appear less extraordinary and more legible.

Mustafa Kemal, as president and founder of both the Turkish Republic and the RPP, remained true to his roots as a Young Turk officer in several important ways. He was, fundamentally, an ardent nationalist with an unswerving commitment to the preservation of the state. Like the CUP before it, his RPP (which was populated by numerous former Young Turk figures) propagated a worldview that placed the precepts of etatism, rationality, secularism, and positivism at the forefront of state policies. An important difference between the CUP and Kemal's RPP can be found in the accent the latter party placed upon nationalism. By the time Atatürk had solidified his standing in office, he and his supporters had begun to solidify and delineate, unquestionably, what it meant to be a Turk and a nationalist; the CUP, by contrast, had never firmly pronounced or defined the content of Ottoman and Turkish nationalism. Nevertheless, the two parties shared a similar approach toward dissent. Neither governing regime proved willing to broker much compromise with those who rejected or deviated from standing state policy. Both governments were willing to use violence to assure that its ends were achieved.

Ideologically, one can see multiple continuities between the ideas harbored by Mustafa Kemal as an imperial officer and the convictions Atatürk championed as president. He, like many Ottoman officers from his generation, possessed an ambivalent relationship with Islam. While the religion did inform how he saw himself politically as a loyal Ottoman citizen, it is clear that he found Islam, as a system of beliefs and rituals, intrinsically irrational and anti-modern. Contemporary Western intellectual trends had a far greater impact upon him (and many of his close associates) when it came to his emerging views on women, popular culture, economics, and ethnicity. The basic underpinnings of the Turkish nationalism he ultimately came to defend as president first began to coalesce within CUP political circles in the years before World War I. Yet it required the events and policies pursued by the Young Turk government during the war, as well as the Nationalist victory during the War of Independence, for this nationalism to acquire a concrete foundation. In other words, Anatolia had to become a land largely devoid of native Christians (as well as a land where non-Turkish-speaking Muslims were cowed into submission) for Kemal to eventually claim that Turkey was a state comprising a singular body of Muslim Turks.

If one holds Atatürk's Turkey up in comparison with other revolutionary states during the interwar period, one sees a number of striking similarities. Despite Woodrow Wilson's aspirations to create a world "safe for democracy," most of the states that existed at the end of World War I possessed strong authoritarian governments. His desire to acquire "great power and authority" (a statement he confided to his diary at Karlsbad) mirrored a standing tendency among many ambitious political leaders from his age. He, like Enver, Talat, and Cemal before him, saw dictatorship as an essential political tool to save the state during trying times. Like Lenin, Mussolini, Stalin, Pilsudski, Cárdenas, and Hitler, he also saw absolute authority as necessary if essential governmental reforms were to be undertaken and fully implemented. The degree to which his RPP monopolized power, to the point of outlawing any and all independent organizations and modes of public expression, was typical of the times.

An even wider base of comparison can be found when one considers the ideological prerogatives Mustafa Kemal advocated and those espoused by other young, revolutionary regimes in the interwar years. Economic nationalism prevailed in a number of newly independent states. The onset of the Great Depression, as well as the seeming economic miracle occurring in Stalin's Soviet Union, pushed Atatürk and many others to raise capital domestically and force society to industrialize on the basis of its own means. In an era defined by the Wilsonian principles of self-determination, recently conceived notions of race, language, and ethno-history found fertile soil in Turkey and elsewhere. It is during this time that the notion of *la raza*, the idea that Latin Americans shared a common racial origin, gained great currency in Mexico and Brazil. Radical language reform, based upon a simplified model grounded in romantic notions of the past as well as modern needs, gripped Soviet Central Asia. A similar process of language development can be found among the gamut of post-imperial states in central and eastern Europe (such as Greece, Serbia, and Romania) as well as among proponents of Zionism. European and Latin American states such as Mexico and the Soviet Union also maintained rigid secular regimes that disestablished the social influence of clerics. As uncomfortable as the comparison may appear, it is hard not to see parallels between Kemalist notions of race and history and the vulgar and bigoted views found in the policies of Germany's National Socialist Party or Japan's fascist junta. All in all, it was the rule of the day that governments sought to transform their respective populations into bodies of citizens that conformed to modern ideals. Harsh forms of government intervention, which entailed such acts as the mass transfer of peoples and the use of armed suppression, was not unique to interwar Turkey.

Lastly, whether one considers him a hero or tyrant, it is clear that Atatürk bore the weight of power like many important political figures. He was unquestionably quite conscious of his own historical significance and chose, time and again, to present himself to the outside world as a marble model embodying the ideals he adopted. A closer look at his personal life demonstrates that he contended with this challenge with some difficulty. While he did enjoy the company of men and women who were personally devoted to him, his desire to retain his authority compelled him to discard many individuals who had helped him realize his political potential. Politics equally impacted his relationship with his family, which included his mother, his children, and his estranged wife. The degree to which he sought out the affection and companionship of the women around him was tempered by political events, his duties as president, and the symbolism the public gleaned from his personal attachments. His death, brought on by his longstanding struggle with alcoholism, bears further witness to the loneliness some of his confidants perceived in him.

A final accounting of Mustafa Kemal's person, particularly his presidency, is difficult to render in complete isolation. Who he was, and what he achieved, cannot be separated from the story of the late Ottoman Empire and the early Turkish Republic. One certainly can attempt to strip away elements of his legend and set him within his local and global historical context. In doing so, one discovers a person who was quite human and whose politics and aspirations were emblematic of his times. However, this does not change the fact that his life was intimately intertwined with government and the people he strove to represent. Atatürk and Turkey remain, in the minds of many, indivisible.

PRIMARY SOURCE EXCERPTS AND STUDY QUESTIONS

THERE ARE SEVERAL THEMES ONE can extrapolate from Mustafa Kemal's life. His maturation as a general and as founding president of the Republic of Turkey embodies a number of intrinsic themes: (1) the transition from empire to nation-state in the modern Middle East; (2) the adaptation and incorporation of modern ideas to contemporary politics and society; (3) the role of communal violence and statism in the making of modern Turkey; and (4) the origins and evolution of Atatürk's cult of personality. The following documents reflect these themes.

I.

The following document is an excerpt from an interview Mustafa Kemal gave in the winter of 1922, shortly before the final battles of the Turkish War of Independence. It represents the first time he publically related stories from his youth, as well as his entrance into the service of the Ottoman military. In this passage, he explains how he received the moniker Kemal (or "perfect" in Arabic).

After a while my mother began to worry because I had remained uneducated. As a result I went to the home of my aunt in Salonika and the decision was made for me to continue school. I enrolled in the civil service school in Salonika. In the school there was a teacher named Kaymak Hafız.

One day while during lessons in my class I fought with another child. There was quite an uproar. The teacher grabbed me and beat me severely. I was very upset. My grandmother thereafter was against me studying at that school and I immediately disenrolled.

There was a man who lived next to us named Sergeant Kadri. He went to Oğlu Ahmet Bey Military School and wore the school uniform. Upon seeing him I longed to wear such clothes. Later I saw military officers in the streets. I understood that I had to enter down path of the military school in order to accede to such esteem.

At that time, my mother came to Salonika. I told her that I wanted to enter the military school. Mother deferred from things related to the military. She strongly opposed me becoming a soldier. After making it clear to her that it was the time the entrance exams were given, I went to the military school and took the exam. In this way it became a fait accompli with respect to my mother.

In school, I was most passionate about mathematics. In a short time I perhaps knew as much almost as the teacher who gave classes to us. I busied myself with questions that were above the level of the class. I wrote the questions and the teacher gave the answers in writing.

My teacher's name was Mustafa. One day he said to me, My son, your name is also Mustafa, just like mine. . . . This can no longer be. Let us establish a difference between us. From this time forward your name shall be Mustafa Kemal. From that time forward my name in fact remained Mustafa Kemal.[1]

II.

Following is an excerpt from Atatürk's famous 1927 speech (the Nutuk) before the annual congress of his Republican Peoples' Party. In leading up to this segment, he poses that leading

1. Sadi Borak and Utkan Kocatürk (eds.), *Atatürk'ün Söylev ve Demeçleri: Tamim ve Telgrafları, Cilt V* (Ankara: Türk Inkılap Tarihi Enstitüsü Yayınları, 1972), 84–85. Translated by Ryan Gingeras.

Ottoman officials were considering the terms of three different possible peace settlements proposed by the victorious powers. In this passage, he explains the reasoning why he rejected the proposals of British protection, an American mandate, and self-determination for each district remaining in the Ottoman Empire.

Gentlemen, I did not think any of these three proposals could be accepted as the correct one, because the arguments and considerations on which they were based were groundless. In reality, the foundations of the Ottoman State were themselves shattered at that time. Its existence was threatened with extermination. All the Ottoman districts were practically dismembered. Only the fatherland, affording protection to a mere handful of Turks, still remained, and it was now suggested also to divide this. Such expression as: the Ottoman State, Independence, Padişah-Caliph, Government—all of them were meaningless words.

Whose existence was it essential to save? And with whose help? And how? Therefore, what could be a serious and correct solution?

In these circumstances, one solution alone was possible, namely, to create a New Turkish State, the sovereignty and independence of which would be unreservedly recognized by the whole world.

This was the solution we adopted before we left Istanbul and which we began to put into action as soon as we set foot on Anatolian soil at Samsun.

These were the most logical and most powerful arguments in support of this resolution:

The main point was that the Turkish nation should live in honor and dignity. Such a condition could only be attained by complete independence. As vital as considerations of wealth and prosperity might be to a nation, if it is deprived of its independence it no longer deserves to be regarded otherwise than as a slave in the eyes of civilized humanity.

To accept a protectorate of a foreign power would signify that we admit lack of human qualities, weakness, and incapacity. Indeed it is impossible to envisage people who have not descended to this degree of abject servitude willingly accepting a foreign master.

But the Turk is both dignified and proud; he is also capable and talented. Such a nation would prefer to perish than subject itself to the life of a slave.

There, Independence or Death![2]

III.

The following is a passage from Civic Knowledge, *a textbook composed by Atatürk and his daughter, Ayşe Afetinan. It was written with the intention of teaching the fundamental principles of the Republic of Turkey. This document is drawn from the section explaining and defining secularism.*

In ignorant times, when civilization was underdeveloped, intellectual and religious freedom was oppressed. Humanity very much suffered from this. The persecution and torture of those who see it proper to be able to think and say the truth by those who wear the guise of religious guardianship will especially remain a blemished tragedy in human history.

In the Turkish Republic, an established religious ceremony is as free as the freedom to choose any orthodox religion; in other words, religious freedom is inviolable. Naturally, religious security and worship will never be against the rule of good society and it will never be made into a political demonstration. The Turkish Republic in no way tolerates, henceforth, those condition[s] like those seen in bygone eras.

2. Mustafa Kemal Atatürk, *The Great Speech* (Ankara: Atatürk Research Center, 2008), 8–9. Translated by Ryan Gingeras.

Also inside the Turkish Republic, determined lodges and tombs have been closed by law. Religious orders have been abolished. Shaykhs, dervishes, courtly titles, caliphs, fortune-tellers, witchcraft and tomb keepers are forbidden because they are sources of reaction and markers of ignorance. The Turkish nation does not tolerate and has not tolerated such institutions and those who comprise them.

Secularism—The Turkish Republic has no official religion. Under the state's administration, all laws and regulations are made and applied in accordance with the world's demands and in according with principles and forms supplied by the science of contemporary civilization. Since religious interpretation is a matter of conscience, the republic sees the separation of religious beliefs from the issues and politics of the state and world as the cardinal element in the success of the contemporary progress of our nation.[3]

❖

IV.

The following is a telegram sent to the people of the southern Turkish town of Gaziantep in commemoration of their liberation from French occupation during the Turkish War of Independence. Formerly known as Ayntab, the town and its surrounding districts had long been home to large numbers of Turks, Armenians, Kurds, Arabs, and other groups before World War I. Sunni Muslim Turkish speakers became the majority population of the town by the time the city assumed the name Gazi Antep ("gazi" being an honorific term in commemoration of the National Forces who participated in the region's resistance to the French).

3. Ayşe Afetinan (ed.), *Medeni Bilgiler ve M. K. Atatürk El Yazıları* (Ankara: Türk Tarih Kurumu, 1969), 56. Translated by Ryan Gingeras.

Fifteen years earlier, Antep, which is only a Turkish city, had fallen in every which way in the hands of foreign forces. This totally Turkish city, without seeing any material support, liberated itself with great heroism and suitably, perfectly secured itself the title Gazi. I regard the people of Gazi Antep with deep respect today as much as that day.

Every city, every town, and the smallest Turkish village that says I am Turkish should take the people of Gaziantep as the model of heroism. [My] delight and happiness is at its highest when I hear it proclaimed that I am personally together with those people who have established with heroism the great wealth of Turkishness in the ancient historical home of the Turks.[4]

K. Atatürk

4. Atatürk'ün Tanim, *Telegraf ve Beyannameleri, IV* (Ankara: Türk Tarih Kurumu Basımevi, 1991), 656–657. Translated by Ryan Gingeras.

STUDY QUESTIONS

1. What aspects of Mustafa Kemal's upbringing, be it his family life, education, or his places of residence, influenced his future political opinions? In what ways did his youth, particularly before he arrived to Istanbul, affect his later political philosophy?

2. Throughout his life, Atatürk struggled with what it meant to be modern and how to apply modern principles to governing both the Ottoman Empire and the Republic of Turkey. Judging from his career and the documents presented here, what were the most important attributes of the modern state and society?

3. Mustafa Kemal is recognized, first and foremost, as Turkey's premier military hero. Why? What aspects of his military service elevated him to such high esteem?

4. In selecting a surname for himself, Mustafa Kemal chose to be called Atatürk or "Father of the Turks." However, assuming a Turkish identity was something that he only gradually came to acquire over the course of his life. Considering what you have read, how did Mustafa Kemal come to think of himself as a Turk?

5. While known for his foresight and vision as a political leader, Atatürk's rule was marked by violence and intolerance for dissent. What aspects of his personality led him to rule in such a way? How did the evolution of the late Ottoman Empire, particularly the events that marked the empire's collapse, influence the harshness of his rule?

6. In looking at both the documents herein and the evolution of his life, how did Mustafa Kemal's cult of personality emerge? What aspects of his life and works have led people to remember him in glowing terms? In what ways did he help orchestrate how people remembered him?

FURTHER READING

RECOMMENDED PRIMARY SOURCES

Afetinan, Ayşe. *Mustafa Kemal Atatürk'ün Karlsbad Hatıraları*. Ankara: Türk Tarih Kurumu, 1991. Representing some of Mustafa Kemal's earliest writings, this volume encapsulates his mood and opinions from World War I.

Afetinan, Ayşe. *Medeni Bilgiler ve M. K. Atatürk El Yazıları*. Ankara: Türk Tarih Kurumu, 1968. Although primarily meant as a textbook, this work encompasses the core philosophy of Ataturk in the 1930s.

Arar, Ismail (ed.). *Atatürk'ün İzmit Basın Toplantısı*. Istanbul: Burçak Yayın,1969. As a long interview, this work gives a good indication of both the direction of his early political leanings and his opinions on World War I and the Turkish War of Independence.

Atatürk, Mustafa Kemal. *The Great Speech*. Ankara: Atatürk Research Center, 2008. Among the few primary sources in English, this rather loose translation of *Atatürk's* famous speech represents only a partial reproduction of what is available in Turkish.

Atatürk, Mustafa Kemal. *Nutuk-Söylev*. Ankara: Türk Tarih Kurumu, 1981. One of many reproductions of Atatürk's 1927 *Nutuk*, complete with the amended documents he references throughout the speech.

Atatürk, Mustafa Kemal. *Atatürk'ün Bütün Eserleri*. Istanbul: Kaynak Yayınları, 1998. The complete works of Atatürk contain thirty volumes of writings with personal notes, speeches, interviews, and other private papers.

Tüfekçi, Gürbüz (ed.). *Atatürk'ün Okuduğu Kitaplar*. Istanbul: Türkiye İş Bankası Kültür Yayınları, 1983. A book that compiles a list of titles of books found in Atatürk's library, as well as handwritten notes and observations that were found in the margins.

RECOMMENDED SECONDARY SOURCES

Armstrong, Harold. *Grey Wolf: The Life of Kemal Ataturk*. New York: Capricorn Books, 1933. The first full-length biography on Mustafa Kemal written in English, it represents a highly salacious contemporary attempt to explain and contextualize the Gazi's life.

Şevket Süreyya Aydemir. *Tek Adam*. Istanbul: Remzi Kitapevi, 2007. This three-volume work remains a standard Turkish language account of Mustafa Kemal's life and times. One of the first produced with the help of primary documents.

Dumont, Paul. *Mustapha Kemal Invente la Turquie Moderne*. Brussels: Editions Complexe, 1983. A concise, critical history of Mustafa Kemal and the birth of the republic until the end of the 1920s.

Gawrych, George. *The Young Atatürk: From Ottoman Soldier to Statesman of Turkey*. London: I.B. Tauris, 2013. Among the more recent biographies to look specifically at the military career of Mustafa Kemal Atatürk.

Hanioğlu, M. Şükrü. *Atatürk: An Intellectual Biography*. Princeton, NJ: Princeton University Press, 2011. As a work that reflects the ideas and intellectual environment of his lifetime and peers, this book provides an essential introduction to the philosophical framework that defined the eventual emergence of Kemalism.

Heper, Metin. *Ismet Inonu: Turkish Democrat and Statesman*. Leiden: Brill, 1998. The only English language biography of Mustafa Kemal's longtime lieutenant and political heir.

Ihrig, Stefan. *Atatürk in the Nazi Imagination*. Cambridge, MA: Belknap Press 2014. As look at Atatürk through the eyes of intellectuals, politicians and artists in Hitler's Germany, this recent work emphasizes the profound influence Kemalism had upon the ideological underpinnings of National Socialism.

Kinross, Patrick. *Atatürk: The Rebirth of a Nation*. London: Phoenix Giant, 1998. Perhaps the most popular Atatürk biography, Kinross's work is the baseline study from which contemporary revisionist surveys have departed.

Kreiser, Klaus. *Atatürk: Eine Biographie.* Munich: Verlag C. H. Beck, 2008. Perhaps the best current account of Atatürk's life available (albeit in German), it reflects most of the current trends in research and interpretation.

Landau, Jacob (ed.), *Atatürk and the Modernization of Turkey.* Leiden, Brill, 1984. Still an indispensable series of essays on the origins, evolution, and implication of Mustafa Kemal's reforms.

Mango, Andrew. *Atatürk: The Biography of the Founder of Modern Turkey.* Woodstock, NY: Overlook Press, 2000. Mango's magnum opus now stands as the most comprehensive revisionist study on Atatürk's life, one that is often considered the most "balanced" of his biographies to date.

MacFie, A. L. *Profiles in Power: Atatürk.* Oxon: Routledge, 2013. A concise, recently re-released biography with heavy emphasis upon the Turkish War of Independence.

Sonyel, Salahi. *Atatürk—The Founder of Modern Turkey.* Ankara: Türk Tarih Kurumu, 1989. As the one English-language biography endorsed and published by the Turkish Historical Association, Sonyel's work reflects many of the tendencies that define pro-Kemalist scholarship.

Volkan, Vamık, and Norman Itzkowitz. *The Immortal Atatürk: A Psychobiography.* Chicago: University of Chicago Press, 1984. As the most critical and personal biography of Atatürk, this book, written by both a historian and a psychiatrist, represents an attempt to diagnose and contextualize Mustafa Kemal's psychological state of mind as it pertains to his political career and private life.

Zürcher, Erik Jan, *The Unionist Factor: The Role of the Committee of Union and Progress in the Turkish Nationalist Movement, 1905–1926.* Leiden: Brill Press, 1984. While not a biography, *Unionist Factor* is the premier work to thoroughly critique and unravel the rise of Mustafa Kemal from the late Ottoman period to his first years as president of the Republic of Turkey.

NOTES

CHAPTER I

1. Klaus Kreiser, *Atatürk: Eine Biographie* (Munich: Verlag C. H. Beck, 2008), p. 23.
2. M. Şükrü Hanioğlu, *Atatürk: An Intellectual Biography* (Princeton, NJ: Princeton University Press, 2011), p. 29.
3. Tahsin Uzer, *Makedonya Eşkiyalık Tarihi ve Son Osmanlı Yönetimi* (Ankara: Türk Tarih Kurumu Basımevi, 1979), p. 84.
4. Andrew Mango, *Atatürk: The Biography of the Founder of Modern Turkey* (Woodstock, NY: Overlook Press, 2000), p. 46.
5. Hanioğlu, *Atatürk*, p. 34.
6. Kemal Karpat, *Politicization of Islam: Reconstructing Identity, State, Faith and Community in the Late Ottoman State* (Oxford: Oxford University Press), p. 334.
7. Vamık Volkan and Norman Itzkowitz, *The Immortal Atatürk: A Psychobiography* (Chicago: University of Chicago Press, 1984), pp. 47–48.
8. Resneli Ahmet Niyazi, *Hürriyet Kahramanı Resneli Niyzai Hatıratı* (Istanbul: Örgün Yayınevi, 2003), p. 191.
9. Ibid.
10. Mango, *Atatürk*, p. 84.
11. A. L. Macfie, *Atatürk* (Essex, UK: Pearson Education Limited, 1994), p. 38.
12. Stavro Skendi, *The Albanian National Awakening, 1878–1912* (Princeton, NJ: Princeton University Press, 1967), p. 405.
13. Mango, *Atatürk*, p. 95.
14. Ibid., p. 108.

CHAPTER 2

1. Patrick Kinross, *Atatürk: The Rebirth of a Nation* (London: Phoenix Giant, 1998), p. 54.
2. Mango, *Atatürk*, p. 142.
3. Ibid., p. 130.
4. Peter Hart, *Gallipoli* (Oxford: Oxford University Press, 2011), pp. 97–98.
5. Kreiser, *Atatürk*, p. 89.
6. Edward Erickson, *Ordered to Die: A History of the Ottoman Army in World War I* (Westport, CT: Greenwood Press, 2001), p. 94.
7. Kreiser, *Atatürk*, pp. 104–105.
8. Mango, *Atatürk*, p. 164.
9. Mustafa Kemal Atatürk, *The Great Speech* (Ankara: Atatürk Research Center, 2008), p. 3.

10. Erik Zürcher, "Renewal and Silence: Postwar Unionist and Kemalist Rhetoric on the Armenian Genocide," in *A Question of Genocide: Armenians and Turks at the End of the Ottoman Empire*, edited by Norman Naimark, Ronald Suny, and Fatma Müge Göçek (Oxford: Oxford University Press, 2011), p. 312.

11. Kreiser, *Atatürk*, p. 108.

12. Uluğ İğdemir, *Atatürk'ün Yaşamı, I Cilt, 1881–1918* (Ankara: Türk Tarih Kurumu Basımevi, 1980), p. 150.

13. Ayşe Afetinan, *Mustafa Kemal Atatürk'ün Karlsbad Hatıraları* (Ankara: Türk Tarih Kurumu, 1991), pp. 43, 49.

14. Mango, *Atatürk*, p. 176.

15. Ibid., p. 181.

16. Nihat Erim, *Devletlerarası Hukuku ve Siyasi Tarih Metinleri, Cilt I* (Ankara: Türk Tarih Kurumu Basımevi, 1953), p. 520.

17. Ahmed Emin Yalman, *Turkey in My Time* (Norman: University of Oklahoma Press, 1956), p. 50.

CHAPTER 3

1. Gazi Mustafa Kemal, *Nutuk-Söylev* (Ankara: Türk Tarih Kurumu, 1981), p. 18.

2. Ibid, p. 902.

3. PRO/FO 371/4161/49194, March 19, 1919.

4. Stanford Shaw, *From Empire to Republic: The Turkish War of National Liberation, 1918–1923: A Documentary Study* (Ankara: Türk Tarih Kurumu Basımevi, 2000), p. 666.

5. Ibid., p. 696.

6. Ibid., p. 697.

7. Andrew Mango, "Ataturk and Kurds," *Middle Eastern Studies* 35, no. 4 (October 1999), p. 10.

8. Shaw, *From Empire to Republic*, p. 803.

9. Ibid.

10. "Kemal Presents Nationalist Views," *New York Times*, May 4, 1920.

11. Shaw, *From Empire to Republic*, p. 977.

12. "Mustafa Kemal Pascha," *Hamburger Nachrichten*, February 12, 1921. Cited in S. Eriş Ülger, *Atatürk und Die Türkei in der deutschen Presse* (1910–1944) (Hückelhoven: Schulbuchverlag Anadolu, 1993, p. 79).

13. "The Stubborn Turk," *The New York Times*, May 5, 1920.

14. PRO/FO 371/5044/1917, March 19, 1920.

15. Charles D. Haley, "A Desperate Ottoman: Enver Pasa and the German Empire," *Middle Eastern Studies* 30, no. 2 (April 1994), p. 10.

16. Michael Llewellyn Smith, *Ionian Vision: Greece in Asia Minor, 1919–1922* (London: Hurst & Company, 1998), p. 245.

17. Şevket Süreyya Aydemir, *Tek Adam: Mustafa Kemal, 1919–1922* (Istanbul: Remzi Kitapevi, 2007), p. 459.

18. Mango, *Atatürk*, p. 346.

CHAPTER 4

1. Volkan and Itzkowitz, *The Immortal Atatürk*, p. 212.
2. Atatürk, *Nutuk-Söylev*, p. 578.
3. Andrew Mango, *From the Sultan to Atatürk* (London: Haus Histories, 2009), p. 151.
4. Sadi Borak and Utkan Kocatürk (eds.), *Atatürk'ün Söylev ve Demeçleri: Tamim ve Telgrafları, Cilt V* (Ankara: Türk Inkılap Tarihi Enstitüsü Yayınları, 1972), p. 98.
5. Ayhan Aktar, "Homogenising the Nation, Turkifying the Economy: The Turkish Experience of Population Exchange Reconsidered," in Renee Hirschon (ed.), *Crossing the Aegean: An Appraisal of the 1923 Compulsory Population Exchange between Greece and Turkey* (New York: Berghan Books, 2008), p. 87.
6. Partick Kinross, *Atatürk: The Rebirth of a Nation* (London: Phoenix Giant, 1998), p. 379.
7. Atatürk, *Nutuk-Söylev*, pp. 654–655.
8. Volkan and Iztkowitz, *The Immortal Atatürk*, p. 217.
9. Ismail Arar (ed.), *Atatürk'ün İzmit Basın Toplantısı* (Istanbul: Burçak Yayın, 1969), p. 41.
10. M. Naeem Qureshi, *Pan-Islam in British Indian Politics: A Study of the Khilafat Movement, 1918–1924* (Leiden: Brill, 1999), p. 368.
11. Atatürk, *Nutuk-Söylev*, p. 661.
12. Ibid., p. 671.
13. http://www.diyanet.gov.tr/english/tanitim.asp?id=13.
14. Borak and Kocatürk, *Atatürk'ün Söylev ve Demeçleri*, p. 107.
15. Ibid, p. 678.
16. Macfie 159.
17. Mango, "Atatürk and Kurds," p. 15.
18. Atatürk, *Nutuk-Söylev*, p. 711.
19. Ibid., pp. 713–714.
20. Ibid., p. 712.
21. Ibid., p. 714.
22. Ibid., 714.

CHAPTER 5

1. Yalman, *Turkey in My Time*, pp. 174–175.
2. Kreiser, *Atatürk*, p. 233.
3. Gürbüz Tüfekçi (ed.), *Atatürk'ün Okuduğu Kitaplar* (Istanbul: Türkiye İş Bankası Kültür Yayınları, 1983), p. 432.
4. Hanioğlu, *Atatürk*, p. 217.
5. Arı İnan (ed.), *Tarihe Tanıklık Edenler: Cumhuriyet Kurucu Kuşağıyla Söyleşiler* (Istanbul: Türkiye Bankası Kültür Yayınları, 2010), p. 127.
6. Ayşe Afetinan (ed.), *Medeni Bilgiler ve M. K. Atatürk El Yazıları* (Ankara: Türk Tarih Kurumu, 1969), p. 19.

7. Paul Dumont, "The Origins of Kemalist Ideology," in Jacob Landau (ed.), *Atatürk and the Modernization of Turkey* (Boulder, CO: Westview Press, 1984), p. 29.

8. Afetinan, *Medeni*, p. 23.

9. Meltem Türköz, "Instrumentalizing Fantasy: The Process of Surname Legislation in the Republic of Turkey 1934–1937," in Gavin D. Brockett (ed.), *Towards a Social History of Modern Turkey: Essays in Theory and Practice* (Istanbul: Libra Press, 2011), p. 72.

10. Wadie Jwaideh, *The Kurdish National Movement: Its Origins and Development* (Syracuse, NY: Syracuse University Press, 2006), p. 214.

11. "'Dersim Katliamı'nda Kimyasal İzi İlk Kez Ortaya Çıktı," *Radikal* 12 April 2013, http://www.radikal.com.tr/turkiye/dersim_katliaminda_kimyasal_izi_ilk_kez_ortaya_cikti-1164486 (consulted 5 May 2015).

12. İnan, *Tarihe Tanıklık Edenler*, p. 85.

13. *Atatürk'ün Tamim, Telgraf ve Beyannameleri, Cilt IV* (Ankara: Türk Tarih Kurumu Basımevi, 1991), p. 643.

14. Afetinan, *Medeni*, p. 114.

15. William Hale, *Turkish Politics and the Military* (London: Routledge, 1994), p. 81.

16. *Atatürk'ün Tamim*, p. 608.

17. "Kemal Atatürk gestorben," *Deutsche Allgemeine Zeitung*, November 11, 1938 (cited in S. Eriş Ülger, *Atatürk und Die Türkei in der deutschen Presse* (1910–1944) (Hückelhoven: Schulbuchverlag Anadolu, 1993, p. 142).

18. Afshin Marashi, "Performing the Nation: The Shah's Official State Visit to Kemalist Turkey, June to July 1934," in Stephanie Cronin (ed.), *The Making of Modern Iran: State and Society under Riza Shah* (London: Routledge, 2003), pp. 111–112.

19. Donald Webster, *The Turkey of Atatürk: Social Process in the Turkish Reformation* (Philadelphia: American Academy of Political and Social Science, 1939), p. 118.

20. Kreiser, *Atatürk*, p. 261.

21. Feroz Ahmad, *The Making of Modern Turkey* (London: Routledge, 2002), p. 88.

22. Mango, *Atatürk*, p. 439.

23. United States National Archive (USNA) Record Group (RG) 59, 867.00/1999, 16 July 1928.

24. USNA, RG 59, 867.001K31/35, 14 March 1929.

25. Salih Bozok and Cemil Bozok, *Hep Atatürk'ün Yanında* (Istanbul: Çağdaş Yayınları, 1985), p. 266.

26. USNA, RG 59, 867.001 Atatrurk, Kamal/75, 15 November 1938.

27. "Gazi Mustafa Kemal Atatürk" *Hamburger Fremdenblatt* 11 November 1938 (cited in S. Eriş Ülger, *Atatürk und Die Türkei in der deutschen Presse* (1910–1944) (Hückelhoven: Schulbuchverlag Anadolu, 1993, p. 142).

28. "Ataturk," *The New York Times*, November 11, 1938.

29. İnan, *Tarihe Tanıklık Edenler*, p. 302.

CHAPTER 6

1. Ernest Jackh, *The Rising Crescent: Turkey Yesterday, Today, and Tomorrow* (New York: Farrar & Rinehart, 1944), p. 198.
2. Yonca Poyraz Doğan, "PM Erdoğan Apologizes over Dersim Massacre on Behalf of Turkish State," *Today's Zaman*, November 23, 2011.

CREDITS

Page 10: Library of Congress Prints and Photographs Division LC-USZ62-66142.

Page 13: Atatürk Research Center Library (Atatürk Araştırma Merkez Kütüphanesi).

Page 22: Atatürk Research Center Library (Atatürk Araştırma Merkez Kütüphanesi).

Page 31: © Chronicle/Alamy, DR9MWD.

Page 47: Atatürk Research Center Library (Atatürk Araştırma Merkez Kütüphanesi).

Page 54: Library of Congress Prints and Photographs Division LC-DIG-ggbain-27083.

Page 63: Library of Congress Prints and Photographs Division LC-USZ62-139313.

Page 82: Atatürk Research Center Library (Atatürk Araştırma Merkez Kütüphanesi).

Page 99: Atatürk Research Center Library (Atatürk Araştırma Merkez Kütüphanesi).

Page 110: www.levantineheritage.com.

Page 124: Atatürk Research Center Library (Atatürk Araştırma Merkez Kütüphanesi).

Page 134: Atatürk Research Center Library (Atatürk Araştırma Merkez Kütüphanesi).

Page 146: Kâzım Karabekir, *İzmir Suikastı*, Emre Yayınları, 5. Baskı-Mayıs/2000, İstanbul, ISBN 975-7369-33-0, p. 303.

Page 153: Atatürk Research Center Library (Atatürk Araştırma Merkez Kütüphanesi).

Page 161: ullstein bild/Contributor/ Getty Images, 541050143.

Page 175: Library of Congress, Prints & Photographs Division, LC-M33-7313 [P&P].

Page 178: Atatürk Research Center Library (Atatürk Araştırma Merkez Kütüphanesi).

INDEX